LITERATURE FROM CRESCENT MOON PUBLISHING

Sexing Hardy: Thomas Hardy and Feminism
by Margaret Elvy

Thomas Hardy's Jude the Obscure: A Critical Study
by Margaret Elvy

Thomas Hardy's Tess of the d'Urbervilles: A Critical Study
by Margaret Elvy

Stepping Forward: Essays, Lectures and Interviews
by Wolfgang Iser

Andrea Dworkin
by Jeremy Mark Robinson

German Romantic Poetry: Goethe, Novalis, Heine, Holderlin
by Carol Appleby

Cavafy: Anatomy of a Soul
by Matt Crispin

Rilke: Space, Essence and Angels in the Poetry of Rainer Maria Rilke
by B.D. Barnacle

Rimbaud: Arthur Rimbaud and the Magic of Poetry
by Jeremy Mark Robinson

Shakespeare: Love, Poetry and Magic in Shakespeare's Sonnets and Plays
by B.D. Barnacle

Feminism and Shakespeare
by B.D. Barnacle

The Poetry of Landscape in Thomas Hardy
by Jeremy Mark Robinson

D.H. Lawrence: Infinite Sensual Violence
by M.K. Pace

D.H. Lawrence: Symbolic Landscapes
by Jane Foster

The Passion of D.H. Lawrence
by Jeremy Mark Robinson

Samuel Beckett Goes Into the Silence
by Jeremy Mark Robinson

In the Dim Void: Samuel Beckett's Late Trilogy:
Company, Ill Seen, Ill Said and Worstward Ho
by Gregory Johns

Andre Gide: Fiction and Fervour in the Novels
by Jeremy Mark Robinson

The Ecstasies of John Cowper Powys
by A.P. Seabright

Amorous Life: John Cowper Powys and the Manifestation of Affectivity
by H.W. Fawkner

Postmodern Powys: New Essays on John Cowper Powys
by Joe Boulter

Rethinking Powys: Critical Essays on John Cowper Powys
edited by Jeremy Mark Robinson

Thomas Hardy and John Cowper Powys: Wessex Revisited
by Jeremy Mark Robinson

Thomas Hardy: The Tragic Novels
by Tom Spenser

Julia Kristeva: Art, Love, Melancholy, Philosophy, Semiotics
by Kelly Ives

Luce Irigaray: Lips, Kissing, and the Politics of Sexual Difference
by Kelly Ives

Helene Cixous I Love You: The Jouissance of Writing
by Kelly Ives

Emily Dickinson: *Selected Poems*
selected and introduced by Miriam Chalk

Petrarch, Dante and the Troubadours: The Religion of Love and Poetry
by Cassidy Hughes

Dante: *Selections From the Vita Nuova*
translated by Thomas Okey

Friedrich Holderlin: *Selected Poems*
translated by Michael Hamburger

Walking In Cornwall
by Ursula Le Guin

Dance the Orange
Selected Poems

Dance the Orange
Selected Poems

Rainer Maria Rilke

Translated by Michael Hamburger
Edited by Jeremy Mark Robinson

CRESCENT MOON

First published 2003. Second edition 2007. Third edition 2012.
Translation © Michael Hamburger 1981, 2003, 2007, 2012.
Introduction © Jeremy Robinson 2003, 2007, 2012.

Printed and bound in the U.S.A.
Design by Radiance Graphics
Set in Book Antiqua 11 on 13pt.

British Library Cataloguing in Publication data

Rilke, Rainer Maria, 1875-1926
Dance the Orange: Selected Poems. – (European Writers)
I. Title II. Robinson, Jeremy Mark
831.9'12

ISBN-13 9781861713667

Crescent Moon Publishing
P.O. Box 1312,
Maidstone, Kent
ME14 5XU, Great Britain
www.crmoon.com

CONTENTS

ACKNOWLEDGEMENTS

To Michael Hamburger; Peter Jay; Insel Verlag, Frankfurt am Main, Germany.

Anvil Press Poetry for permission to reprint from Michael Hamburger's translations of Rainer Maria Rilke, which are taken from *An Unofficial Rilke: Poems 1912-1926,* Anvil Press Poetry, 1981, and Michael Hamburger, *Collected Poems, 1941-1994,* Anvil Press Poetry, 1995.

DANCE THE ORANGE

SELECTED POEMS

Rainer Maria Rilke
by Paula Modersohn-Becker,
1906 (right).

Rainer Maria Rilke and Clara Westhoff in 1904

DER GEIST ARIEL

Nach der Lesung con Shakespeares Sturm

Man hat ihn einmal irgendwo befreit
mit jenem Ruck, mit dem man sich als Jüngling
ans Große hinriß, weg von jeder Rücksicht.
Da ward er willens, sieh: und seither dient er,
nach jeder Tat gefaßt auf seine Freiheit.
Und halb sehr herrisch, halb beinah verschämt,
bringt man ihm vor, daß man für dies und dies
ihn weiter brauchte, ach, und muß es sagen,
was man ihm half. Und dennoch fühlt man selbst,
wie alles das, was man mit ihm zurückhält,
fehlt in der Luft. Verführend fast und süß:
ihn hinzulassen –, um dann, nicht mehr zaubernd,
ins Schicksal eingelassen wie die andern,
zu wissen, daß sich seine leichte Freundschaft,
jetzt ohne Spannung, nirgends mehr verpflichtet,
ein Überschuß zu dieses Atmens Raum,
gedankenlos im Element beschäftigt.
Abhängig fürder, länger nicht begabt,
den dumpfen Mund zu jenem Ruf zu formen,
auf den er stürzte. Machtlos, alternd, arm
und doch *ihn* atmend wie unfaßlich weit
verteilten Duft, der erst das Unsichtbare
vollzählig macht. Auflächelnd, daß man dem
so winken durfte, in so großen Umgang
so leicht gewöhnt. Aufweiend vielleicht auch,
wenn man bedenkt, wie's einen liebte und
fortwollte, beides, immer ganz in Einem.

(Ließ ich es schon? Nun shreckt mich dieser Mann,
der wieder Herzog wird. Wie er sich sanft
den Draft ins Haupt zieht und sich zu den andern
Figuren hängt und künftighin das Spiel
um Milde bittet… Welcher Epilog

vollbrachter Herrschaft. Abtun, bloßes Dastehn
mit nichts als eigner Kraft: «und das ist wenig.»)

(1913)

«UNWISSEND VOR DEM HIMMEL MEINES LEBENS»

Unwissend vor dem Himmel meines Lebens,
anstaunend steh ich. O die großen Sterne.
Aufgehendes und Niederstieg. Wie still.
Als wär ich nicht. Nehm ich denn Teil? Entriet ich
dem reinen Einfluß? Wechselt Flut und Ebbe
in meinem Blut nach dieser ordnung? Abtun
will ich die Wünsche, jeden andern Anschluß,
mein Herz gewöhnen an sein Fernstes. Besser
es lebt im Schrecken seiner Sterne, als
zum Schein beschützt, von einer Näh beschwichtigt.

(1913)

CHRISTI HÖLLENFAHRT

Endlich verlitten, entging sein Wesen dem schrecklichen
Leibe der Leiden. Oben. Ließ ihn.
Und die Finsternis fürchtete sich allein
und warf an das Bleiche
Fledermäuse heran, – immer noch schwankt abends
in ihrem Flattern die Angst vor dem Anprall
an die erkaltete Qual. Dunkle ruhlose Luft
entmutigte sich an dem Leichnam; und in den starken
wachsamen Tieren der Nacht war Dumpfheit und Unlust.
Sein entlassener Geist gedachte vielleicht in der Landschaft
anzustehen, unhandelnd. Denn seiner Leidung Ereignis
war noch genug. Maßvoll
schien ihm der Dinge nächtliches Dastehn,
und wie ein trauriger Raum griff er darüber um sich.
Aber die Erde, vertrocknet im Durst seiner Wunden,
aber die Erde riß auf, und es rufte im Abgrund.
Er, Kenner der Martern, hörte die Hölle
herheulend, begehrend Bewußtsein
seiner vollendeten Not: daß über dem Ende der seinen
(unendlichen) ihre, währende Pein erschrecke, ahne.
Und er stürzte, der Geist, mit der völligen Schwere
seiner Erschöpfung herein: schrift als ein Eilender
durch das befremdete Nachschaun weidender Schatten,
hob zu Adam den Aufblick, eilig,
eilte hinab, schwand, schien und verging in dem Stürzen
wilderer Tiefen. Plötzlich (höher höher) über der Mitte
auschäumender Schreie, auf dem langen
Turm seines Duldens trat er hervor: ohne Atem,
stand, ohne Geländer, Eigentümer der Schmerzen. Schweig.

(1913)

WENDUNG

Der Weg von der Innigkeit zur Größe geht durch das Opfer.
  Rudolf Kassner

Lange errang ers im Anschaun.
Sterne brachen ins Knie
unter dem ringenden Aufblick.
Oder er anschaute knieend,
und seines Instands Duft
machte ein Göttliches müd,
daß es ihm lächelte schlafend.

Türme schaute er so,
daß sie erschraken:
wieder sie bauend, hinan, plötzlich, in Einem!
Aber wie oft, die vom Tag
überladene Landscaft
ruhete hin in sein stilles Gewahren, abends.

Tiere traten getrost
in den offenen Blick, weidende,
und die gefangenen Löwen
starrten hinein wie in unbegreifliche Freiheit;
Vögel durchflogen ihn grad,
den gemütigen; Blumen
wiederschauten in ihn
groß wie in Kinder.

Und das Gerücht, daß ein Schauender sei,
rührte die minder,
fraglicher Sichtbaren,
rührte die Frauen.

Schauend wie lang?

Seit wie lange schon innig entbehrend,
flehend im Grunde des Blicks?

Wenn er, ein Wartender, saß in der Fremde; des Gasthofs
zerstreutes, abgewendetes Zimmer
mürrisch um sich, und im vermiedenen Spiegel
wieder das Zimmer
und später vom quälenden Bett aus
wieder:
da beriets in der Luft,
unfaßbar beriet es
über sein fühlbares Herz,
über sein durch schmerzhaft verschütteten Körper
dennoch fühlbares Herz
beriet es und richtete:
daß es der Liebe nicht habe.

(Und verwehrte ihm weitere Weihen.)

Denn des Anschauns, siehe, ist eine Grenze.
Und die geschautere Welt
will in der Liebe gedeihn.

Werk des Gesichts ist getan,
tue nun Herz-Werk
an den Bildern in dir, jenen gefangenen; denn du
überwältigtest sie: aber nun kennst du sie nicht.
Siehe, innerer Mann, dein inneres Mädchen,
dieses errungene aus
tausend Naturen, dieses
erst nur errungene, nie
noch geliebte Geschöpf.

(1914)

KLAGE

Wem willst du klagen, Herz? Immer gemiedener
ringt sich dein Weg durch die unbegreiflichen
Menschen. Mehr noch vergebens vielleicht,
da er die Richtung behält,
Richtung zur Zukunft behält,
zu der verlorenen.

Früher. Klagest? Was wars? Eine gefallene
Beere des Jubels, unreife.
Jetzt aber bricht mir mein Jubel-Baum,
bricht mir im Sturme mein langsamer
Jubel-baum.
Schönster in meiner unsichtbaren
Landschaft, der du mich kenntlicher
machtest Engeln, unsichtbaren.

(1914)

AN HOLDERLIN

Verwilung, auch am Vertrautesten nicht,
ist uns gegeben; aus den erfüllenden
Bilden stürzt der Geist zu plötzlich zu füllenden; Seen
sind erst im Ewigen. Hier ist Fallen
das Tüchtigste. Aus dem gekonnten Gefühl
überfallen hinab ins geahndete, weiter.

Dir, du Herrlicher, war, dir war, du Beschwörer, ein ganzes
Leben das dringende Bild, wenn du es aussprachst,
die Zeile schloß sich wie Schicksal, ein Tod war
selbst in der lindesten, und du betratest ihn; aber
der vorgehende Gott führte dich drüben hervor.

O du wandelnder Geist, du wandelndster! Wie sie doch alle
wohnen im warmen Gedicht, häuslich, und lang
bleiben im schmalen Vergleich. Teilnehmende. Du nur
ziehst wie der Mond. Und unten hellt und verdunkelt
deine nächtliche sich, die helig erschrokene Landschaft,
die du in Abschieden fühlst. Keiner
gab sie erhabener hin, gab sie ans Ganze
heiler zurück, unbedürftiger. So auch
spieltest du helig durch nicht mehr gerechnete Jahre
mit dem unendlichen Glück, als wär es nicht innen, läge
keinem gehörend im sanften
Rasen der Erde umher, von göttlichen Kindern verlassen.
Ach, was die Höchsten begehren, du legtest es wunschlos
Baustein auf Baustein: es stand. Doch selber sein Umsturz
irrte dich nicht.

Was, da ein solcher, Ewiger, war, mißtraun wir
immer dem Irdischen noch? Statt am Verläufigen ernst
die Gefühle zu lernen für welche

Neigung, künftig im Raum?

(1914)

«NICHT DAß UNS, DA WIR (PLÖTZLICH) ERWACHSEN SIND»

Nicht daß uns, da wir (plötzlich) erwachsen sind
und plötzlich mit-schuldig an unvor-
denklicher Schuld der Erwachsenen; Mitwisser plötzlich
aller Gewissen –, nicht daß uns dann ein Häscher errät
und handfest hinüber zerrt und zurück
ins vergangne Gefängnis, wo von der Zeit nur
Abwässer sind, die weggeschüttete Zukunft,
draus eine Welle manchmal mit fast ihm
entgangener Hand der Gefangene aufhebt, sie über den
                                        kahlge-
schorenen Kopf hinschüttend wie irgendein Kommen,
––––––––––––––––––––
das nicht [ist unser Ärgstes,]; sondern die Kerker von früh an
die sich aus unserem Atem bilden, aus einer zu zeitig
verstandenen Hoffnung, aus selber
unserem Schicksal. Aus der noch eben
rein durchdringlichen offenen Luft, aus jedem Geschauten.

Wie so mag ein Mädchen auf einmal durch Gitter
seiner Noch-Kindheit den Liebbaren sehn, getrennter
als in Legende. Ihm gegenüber
aufschaun, um ihns Verfrauliche traurig
abzugleiten von ihm.
Oder Getrennten sind mehr. Jahrzehnt und Jahrtausend
von Gesicht zu Gesicht. Und zwischen Erkannten
steht vielleicht im Kerker der Kindheit das besser,
das unendlich berechtigte Herz.

[Mann, sei wie ein Engel,
wenn die Begegnung geschieht und es geht noch das
                                        Mädchen
eingelassen einher im Gleichnis der Kindheit.

[Nicht ein Begehrender, welcher bestünde.]
Sei wie ein Engel. Laß sie nicht rückwärts. Weiter
gieb ihr die Freiheit. Über das bloße
Lieben gieb ihr die Gnade der Liebe. Bewußtsein
gieb ihr der Ströme. Kühnheit der Himmel
stürze um sie. Durch den empfundenen Herzraum
wirf ihr die Vögel]
[Kerker unsägliche, unvermutete Kerker]

(1916)

AN DIE MUSIK

Musik. Atem der Statuen. Vielleicht:
Stille der Bilder. Du Sprache wo Sprachen
enden. Die Zeit,
die senkrecht steht auf der Richtung vergehender Herzen.

Gefühle zu wem? O due der Gefühle
Wandlung in was? –: in hörbare Landschaft.
Du Fremde: Musik. Du uns entwachsener
Herzraum. Innigstes unser,
das, uns übersteigend, hunausdrängt, –
heiliger Abscheid:
da uns das Innre umsteht
als geübteste Ferne, als andre
Seite der Luft:
rein,
riesig,
nicht mehr bewohnbar.

(1914)

GEGEN-STROPHEN

Oh, daß ihr ihier, Frauen, einergeht,
hier unter uns, leidvoll,
nicht geschonter als wir und dennoch imstande,
selig zu machen wie Selige.

Woher,
wenn der Geliebte erscheint,
nehmt ihr die Zukunft?
Mehr, als je sein wird.
Wer die Entfernungen weiß
bis zum äußersten Fixstern,
staunt, wenn er diesen gewahrt,
eurern herrlichen Herzraum.
Wie, im Gedräng, spart ihr ihn aus?
Ihr, voll Quellen und Nacht.

Seid ihr wirklich die gleichen,
die, da ihr Kind wart,
unwirsch im Schulgang
anstieß der ältere Bruder?
Ihr Heilen.

   Wo wir als Kinder uns schon
   Häßlich für immer verzerrn,
   wart ihr wie Brot vor der Wandlung.

Abbruch der Kindheit
war euch nicht Schaden. Auf einmal
standet ihr da, wie im Gott
plötzlich zum Wunder ergänzt.

   Wir, wie gebrochen vom Berg,
   oft schon als Knaben scharf

an den Rändern, vielleicht
manchmal glücklich behaun;
wir, wie Stücke Gesteins,
über Blumen gestürzt.

Blumen des tieferen Erdreichs,
von allen Wurzeln geliebte,
ihr, der Eurydike Schwestern,
immer voll heiliger Umkehr
hinter dem steigenden Mann.

Wir, von uns selber gekränkt,
Kränkende gern und gern
Wiedergekränkte aus Not.
Wir, wie Waffen, dem Zorn
neben den Schlaf gelegt.

Ihr, die ihr beinah Schutz seid, wo niemand
schützt. Wie ein schattiger Schlafbaum
ist der Gedanke an euch
für die Schwärme des Einsamen.

•

Wir, in den ringenden Nächten,
wir fallen von Nähe zu Nähe;
und wo die Liebende taut,
sind wir ein stürzender Stein.

(1912-1922)

SONNET II, 4
from Sonette an Orpheus

O dieses ist das Tier, das nicht giebt.
Sie wußtens nicht und habens jeden Falls
– sein Wandeln, seine haltung, seinen Hals,
bis in des stillen Blickes Licht – geliebt.

Zwar *war* es nicht. Doch weil sie's liebten, ward
ein reines Tier. Sie ließen immer Raum.
Und in dem Raume, klar und ausgespart,
erhob es leicht sein Haupt und brachte kaum

zu sein. Sie nährten es mit keinem Korn,
nur immer mit der Möglichkeit, es sei.
Und die gab solche Stärke an das tier,

daß es aus sich ein Stirnhorn trieb. Ein Horn.
Zu einer Jungfrau kam es weiß herbei –
und war im Silber-Spiegel und in ihr.

(1922)

MAUSOLEUM

Königsherz. Kern eines hohen
Herrscherbaums. Balsamfrucht.
Goldene Herznuß. Urnen-Mohn
mitten im Mittelbau,
(wo der Widerhall abspringt,
wie ein Splitter der Stille,
wenn du dich rührst,
weil es dir scheint,
daß deine vorige
Haltung zu laut war...)
Völkern entzogenes,
sterngesinnt,
im unsichbaren Kreisen
kreisendes Königsherz.

Wo ist, wohin,
jenes der leichten
Lieblingin?
: Lächeln, von außen,
auf die zögernde Rundung
heiterer Früchte gelegt;
oder der Motte, vielleicht,
Kostbarkeit, Florflügel, Fühler...

Wo aber, wo, das sie sang,
das sie in Eins sang,
das Dichterherz?
: Wind,
unsichtbar,
Windinnres.
(1924)

«NACHT. OH DU IN TIEFE GELOSTES»

Nacht. Oh du in Tiefe gelöstes
Gesicht an meinem Gesicht.
Du, meines staunenden Anschauns größtes
Übergewicht.

Nacht, in meinem Blicke erschauernd,
aber in sich so fest;
unerschöpfliche Schöpfung, dauernd
über dem Erdenrest;

voll von jungen Gestirnen, die Feuer
aus der Flucht ihres Saums
schleudern ins lautlose Abenteuer
des Zwischenraums:

wie, durch dein bloßes Dasein, erschein ich,
Übertrefferin, klein –;
doch, mit der dunkelen Erde einig,
wag ich es, in dir zu sein.

(1924)

SCHWERKRAFT

Mitte, wie du aus allen
dich ziehst, auch noch aus Fliegenden dich
wiedergewinnst, Mitte, du Stärkste.

Stehender: wie ein Trank den durst
durchstürzt ihn die Schwerkraft.

Doch aus dem Schlafenden fällt,
wie aus lagernder Wolke,
reichlicher Regen der Schwere.

(1924)

«VON NAHENDEM REGEN FAST ZÄRTLICH VERDUNKELTER GARTEN»

Von nahendem Regen fast zärtlich verdunkelter Garten,
Garten unter der zögernden Hand.
Als besännen sich, ernster, in den Beeten die Arten,
wie es geschah, daß sie ein Gärtner erfand.

Denn sie denken ja ihn; gemischt in die heitere Freiheit
bleibt sein bemühtes Gemüt, bleibt vielleicht sein Verzicht.
Auch an ihnen zerrt, die uns so seltsam erzieht, diese
                                    Zweiheit;
noch in dem Leichtesten wecken wie Gegengewicht.

(1926)

ANKUNFT

In einer Rose steht dein Bett, Geliebte. Dich selber
(oh ich Schwimmer wider die Strömung des Dufts)
has ich verloren. So wie dem Leben zuvor
diese (von außen nicht meßbar) dreimal drei Monate sind,
so, nach innen geschlagen, werd ich erst *sein*. Auf einmal,
zwei Jahrtausende vor jenem neuen Geschöpf,
das wir genießen, wenn die Berüchrung beginnt,
plötzlich: gegen dir über, werd ich im Auge bgeboren.

(1926)

«KOMM DU, DU LETZTER, DEN ICH ANERKENNE»

Komm du, du letzter, den ich anerkenne,
heilloser Schmerz im leiblichen Geweb:
wie ich im Geiste brannte, sieh, ich brenne
in dir; das Holz hat lange widerstrebt,
der flamme, die du loderst, zuzustimmen,
nun aber nähr' ich dich und brenn in dir.
Mein hiesig Mildsein wird in deinem Grimmen
ein Grimm der Hölle nicht von hier.
Ganz rein, ganz planlos frei von Zukunft stieg
ich auf des Leidens wirren Scheiterhaufen,
so sicher nirgend Künftiges zu jaufen
um dieses herz, darin der Vorrat schwieg.
Bin ich es noch, der da unkenntlich brennt?
Erinnenerungen reiß ich nicht herein.
O Leben, Leben: Draußensein.
Und ich in Lohe. Neimand der mich kennt.

[Verzicht. Das ist nicht so wie Krankeit war
einst in der Kindheit. Aufschub. Vorwand um
größer zu werden. Alles rief und raunte.
Misch nicht in dieses was dich früh erstaunte]

(1926)

«ROSE, OH REINER WIDERSPRUCH»

Rose, oh reiner Widerspruch, Lust,
Niemandes Schlaf zu sein unter soviel
Lidern.

(1925)

TRANSLATIONS

THE SPIRIT ARIEL

After reading Shakespeare's The Tempest

At some time somewhere he was liberated
with such a jerk as being young one used
to rip oneself towards greatness, away from stint.
He willed it then; and ever since has served,
ready for freedom after every deed.
Half very masterfully, half almost embarrassed,
one put it to him that for this and that
he's needed still, oh, and has to tell him
how he was helped. And yet one is aware
how all one uses him to keep away
deprives the air. Almost it's tempting, sweet
to let him go –, and then, abjuring magic,
enrolled in destiny like all the others,
to know his easy friendship from now on,
rid of all tension, of all obligation,
a bonus to the ambit of this breathing,
busies itself in the element at random.
Henceforth dependent, no longer with the gift
of shaping a dull mouth into that call
which brought him down. Powerless, aging, poor,
yet breathing *him* like an impalpably far
fragrance, diffused, by which alone the invisible
becomes complete. And smiling at the thought
that one could summon him so, so lightly lean
on such great intercourse. And weeping too
perhaps to think how then it loved one and
longed to escape, both urges always one.

(Have I released it? Now he frightens me,
this man turned Duke again. How gently now
through his own head he threads the wire and hangs
himself up with the other figures and henceforth
begs the play's indulgence... What an epilogue

to mastery achieved. A stripping, mere standing there
with none but his own strength, "which is most faint.")

"IGNORANT I CONFRONT THE HEAVEN OF MY LIFE"

Ignorant I confront the heaven of my life,
wondering at it, I stand. O the great stars.
The rising and the going down. How still.
As though I were not. Am I part of it?
Or have I lost it, severed the pure influx?
Does the same order make
the high and low tides alternate in my blood?
All craving I'll discard, all other connection,
attune my heart to its remotest wave.
Much better to live in terror of its stars
than seemingly pampered, soothed by a nearness.

CHRIST'S DESCENT INTO HELL

Beyond it at last, his being escaped from the terrible
body of torments. Above. Left him.
And the dark, all alone, was afraid
and against the pallor
threw bats, in whose nightfall fluttering even now
wavers the fear of colliding
with an anguish grown cold. The dull, restless air
lost courage in face of the corpse; and a listlessness, a
                                        distaste
filled the sturdy, wakeful creatures of night.
Dismissed, his spirit perhaps thought of lingering
in the landscape, inactive. For the event of his passion
was still enough. Measured
it seemed to him, the nocturnal standing-there
of things: like a sad space he groped round it.
But the earth, parched in the thirst of his wounds,
but the earth burst open, and something called from the
                                        chasm.
He, expert in pains, heard Hell
howl at him, craving awareness
of his accomplished anguish: that through the end of his
(infinite) torture its own, in progress, might be frightened
                                        and guess.
And he plunged, the spirit, into it with the full weight
of his exhaustion: walked as one hurrying
through the astonished stares of pasturing shades,
raised his gaze to Adam, in haste,
hurried down, vanished, shone and went out in the falling
of wilder depths. All at once (higher, higher) over the midst
of shrieks foaming up, on the tall
tower of his suffering he stepped forth: without breath,
stood with no railing to clutch, agony's owner, in silence.

TURNING-POINT

The way from intense inwardness to greatness leads through sacrifice.

   Rudolf Kassner

Long he had won it by looking.
Stars would fall on their knees
under his strenuous up-glance.
Or he would look at it kneeling,
and his urgency's odour
made a divine being tired
so that it smiled at him, sleeping.

Towers he would gaze at so
that they were startled:
building them up again, suddenly, sweeping them up!
But how often the landscape
overburdened by day
ebbed to rest in his quiet perceiving, at nightfall.

Animals trustingly stepped
into his open gaze, grazing ones,
even the captive lions
stared in, as though into incomprehensible freedom;
birds flew through it unswerving,
it that could feel them; and flowers
met and returned his gaze,
great as in children.

And the rumour that here was a seeing man
moved the more faintly,
dubiously visible,
moved the women.

Seeing how long?
How long profoundly deprived,

beseeching deep down in his glance?

When he, a waiting one, sat in strange towns; the hotel's
distracted, preoccupied bedroom
morose about him, and in the avoided mirror
that room once more
and later, from the tormenting bedstead
once more:
then in the air it pronounced,
beyond his grasping pronounced
on his heart that was still to be felt,
through his painfully buried body,
on his heart nonetheless to be felt,
something pronounced then, and judged:
that it was lacking in love.

(And forbade him further communions.)

For looking, you see, has a limit.
And the more looked-at world
wants to be nourished by love.

Work of seeing is done,
now practise heart-work
upon those images captive within you; for you
overpowered them only: but now do not know them.
Look, inward man, look at your inward maiden,
her the laboriously won
from a thousand natures, at her the
being till now only
won, never yet loved.

COMPLAINT

To whom, heart, would you complain? Ever more
                              unfrequented
your war grapples on through incomprehensible
human kind. All the more vainly perhaps
for keeping to its direction,
direction towards the future,
the future that's lost.

Before. You complained? What was it? A fallen
berry of joy, an unripe one.
But now it's my tree of joy that is breaking,
what breaks in the gale is my slow
tree of joy.
Loveliest in my invisible
landscape, you that brought me more close to the
ken of angels, invisible.

TO HÖLDERLIN

To stay, among things most familiar even,
we are not permitted; from the image fulfilled
our minds too suddenly rush into those to be filled; there are
no lakes till eternity. Here
falling's the best we can do: tumble over
from the mastered feeling into the guessed at, onward.

To you, glorious one, who adjured it, for you a whole life
was the urgent image, when you pronounced it
the line closed like a fate, in your gentlest even
a death inhered and you entered it; but
the god walking ahead led you out and across.

You roaming spirit, more roaming than any! How all those
                                        others
are at home in their snug, warm poems, house-proud, and
                                        linger
in narrow analogies. Interested parties. You only
move like the moon. And, below, it lights up and darkens,
your nocturnal landscape, the sacredly startled
which through leave-taking you perceive. No one
gave it away more nobly, gave it back
to the whole more undamaged, more undemandingly. So
too for years no longer counted devoutly you played
with infinite joy, as though it were not inside us
but, belonging to none, lay about
in the tender grass of this earth, left behind by celestial
                                        children.
Oh, what the best aspire to, you, undesiring, laid
brick upon brick: it stood up. But its very collapse
left you composed.

How, after one so timeless has been, can we
still mistrust the earthly? Rather than earnestly learning
from provisional things the feelings for what
inclination to come, in space?

"NOT THAT, WHEN (SUDDENLY) WE ARE GROWN-UP"

Not that, when (suddenly) we are grown-up
and suddenly share the immemorial
guilt of the grown-up; conniving, suddenly,
in everyone's conscience –, not that then a bailiff suspects us
and by force drags us over and back
to the past prison cell, where there's nothing of time
but its effluents, a future poured down the drain
from which the prisoner with a hand that's almost escaped
                                        him
scoops a wavelet from time to time, letting it run
over his shaven head like something that's happening,
----
not *that* [is our worst];[1] but the cells from an early age
that form out of our breathing, out of a
hope too soon understood, out of our very
destinies. Out of the only a moment ago
still purely penetrable open air, out of everything looked at.

So might a girl all at once through the bars of her
childhood not yet outgrown catch sight of a
lovable one, more separate than in legends.
Facing him, look up, to slide off him sadly
into pre-womanhood.
O there are more so separate. Decade, millennium
between face and face. And between those who know each
                                        other
still in the cell of childhood they could be lying,
their more, their endlessly justified hearts.

[Man, be like an angel[2]
when the encounter occurs and the girl walks about
still mirrored in her childhood's metaphor.
[Not a desiring one, out to win.]
Be like an angel. Don't leave her behind you. Continue
to give her that freedom. Beyond

mere loving give her the mercy of love. Give her
awareness of rivers. Around her heap the
boldness of skies. Through the heart-space perceived
throw her the birds]
[Cells unspeakable, unexpected cells]

TO MUSIC

Music: breathing of statues. Perhaps
stillness of pictures. You language where languages
end. You time
that stands perpendicular on the course of transient hearts.

Feelings for whom? O you the mutation
of feelings to what? –: to audible landscape.
You stranger: music. You heart-space
grown out of us. Innermost of us
that, rising above us, seeks the way out –
holy departure:
when what is inward surrounds us
as the most mastered distance, as
the other side of the air:
pure,
immense,
beyond habitation.

ANTISTROPHES

Oh, that you walk about, women,
here in our midst, suffering,
not more spared than we are, yet able
to grant bliss like the blessed.

Where,
when your loved one appears,
do you find so much future?
More than will ever be.
One who knows the distances
up to the farthest of fixed stars
marvels when he observes it,
this your glorious heart-space.
How, in the bustle, do you leave it open?
You, full of wellsprings and night.

Are you really the same
whom as children,
going to school, your big brothers
gruffly barged into, pushed?
You hale ones.

   Where already as children
   we hideously warp for ever,
   you were like bread before changing.

Childhood's breaking-off
did you no harm. All at once
you stood there, completed
as in a god, to a miracle.

   We, as though chipped from the mountain,
   often as boys even sharp
   at the edges, at times
   perhaps happily hewn;
   we, like bits of rock

hurled on to flowers.

Flowers of the deeper earth levels,
loved by all roots,
you, Eurydice's sisters,
always full of holy conversion
behind the ascending man.

We, hurt by ourselves,
keen to hurt and keen
to be hurt in return in our neediness.
We, like weapons laid
beside sleep, for anger.

You that are almost protection, where no one
protects. Like a shady sleep-tree
is the thought of you
for the crowds of lonely men.

•

We, in the grappling nights,
we fall from nearness to nearness;
and where the loving girl thaws
we hurtle down, stones.

SONNET II, 4
from Sonnet to Orpheus

This is the non-existent animal.
Not knowing that, they loved it, loved its ways,
its neck, its posture, loved its quiet gaze
down to the light within it, loved it all.

True, it was *not*. But, because loved, a pure
beast came to be. A space was kept, conceded.
And in that space, left blank for it, secure,
it gently raised its head and hardly needed

to be. They fed it on no kind of corn,
but always only with the right to be.
And on the beast such power this could confer,

its brow put forth new growth. A single horn.
White, it sought out a virgin's company –
and was inside the mirror and in her.

MAUSOLEUM

King's heart. Core of a high
tree of dominion. Balm fruit.
Golden heart-nut. Urn-poppy-seed
in the central tract's centre,
(where the resonance breaks away
like a splinter of stillness
when you stir
because you feel
that your earlier
stance was too noisy...)
king's heart
extracted from peoples,
star-minded,
circling in
its invisible orbit.

Where is, gone where,
that of the light
girl, his love?
: smile, laid from outside
on the hesitant roundness
of carefree fruit;
or the moth, perhaps,
preciousness, gauze-wing, feeler...

Where, though, what sang her,
what sang her into oneness,
the poet's heart?
: wind,
invisible,
wind's interior.

"NIGHT. O FACE AGAINST MY FACE"

Night. O face against my face
dissolved into deepness.
You my marvelling look's most immense
preponderance.

Night, in my gaze a spasm,
in yourself made so fast;
inexhaustible genesis, outlasting
earthly remains;

full of young planets that hurl
fire from the flight of their seams
into the soundless adventure
of the space between:

by your mere existence, exceeder,
how small I grow –;
but at one with the darkened earth
I dare be in you.

GRAVITY

Centre, how from them all
you draw yourself, even from flying creatures
win back yourself, centre, the strongest.

The standing man: as drink through thirst
gravity rushes through him.

But from the sleeper falls,
as from a cloud at rest,
gravity's plentiful rain.

"GARDEN, TENDERLY DARKENED, ALMOST, BY NEARNESS OF RAIN OR THUNDER"

Garden, tenderly darkened, almost, by nearness of rain or
                                        thunder,
garden under hesitant hands.
As though in their beds more earnestly plants now must
                                        wonder
how it could be that a gardener invented their kinds.

For it's of him they are thinking; admixed to pure freedom,
                                      their trueness,
to them his laborious care, or acceptance or failure, clings.
Even they feel the pull of our curious tutor, that twoness;
we awaken the counterweight in the very lightest of things.

ARRIVAL

Inside a rose your bed stands, beloved. Your very self
(oh, I the swimmer against the current of fragrance)
I have lost. As to my life before now
these (from outside uncountable) three times three months
                                              are,
so, beaten inward, not till then shall I *be*. All at once,
two millennia before that new creature
whom we enjoy when the touching begins,
suddenly: faced with you, I am born, in the eye.

"NOW COME, THE LAST THAT I CAN RECOGNIZE"

Now come, the last that I can recognize,
pain, utter pain, fierce in the body's texture.
As once in the mind I burned, so now I burn
in you; the wood resisted, long denied
acceptance to the flame you blazed at me,
but now I feed you and in you I flare.
My mildness here in your hot rage must turn
to hellish rage, hell-fury, kindled there.
Quite pure of forethought, futureless and free
I mounted suffering's tangled, criss-crossed pyre,
so sure there was no purchase to acquire
for this heart's future, all its store now silent.
What burns there, so transmuted, is that I?
Into this fire I drag no memory.
To be alive, alive: to be outside.
And I ablaze. With no one who knows me.

[Renunciation. Not what illness was
in childhood once. Postponement. Pretext for
a growing-up. When all things called, urged on.
That early wonderment, keep it out of this]

"ROSE, PURE CONTRADICTION, DELIGHT"

Rose, pure contradiction, delight
in being nobody's sleep under so many
eyelids.

(Rilke's epitaph)

Illustrations

Rainer Maria Rilke
by Maler Helmut Westoff (above).

Rilke at the Hotel Biron, Paris
(above), and in 1897 (left).

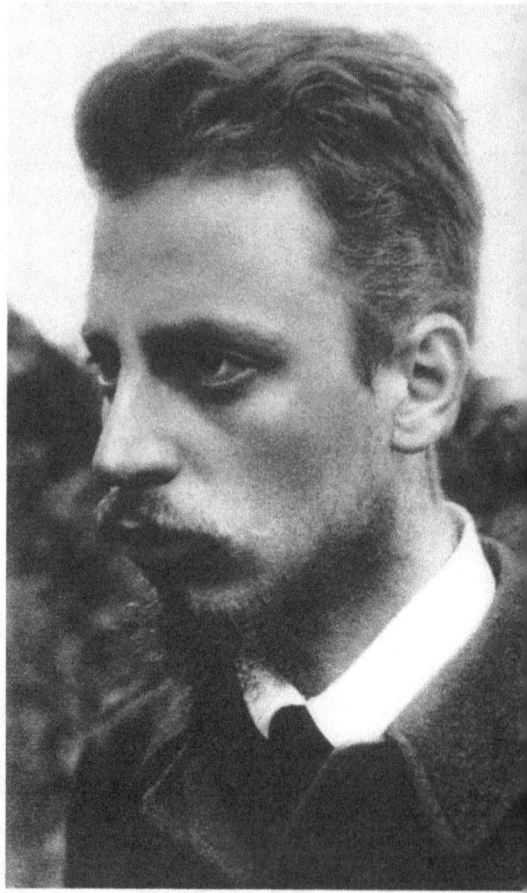

Lou Andreas-Salomé

Notes On the Poems

Please also refer to the Bibliography

Der Geist Ariel, The Spirit Ariel

Written in Ronda, Spain, around the same time as 'The Spanish Trilogy', after Rainer Maria Rilke had read William Shakespeare's *The Tempest* for the first time in early 1913.

«*Unwissend vor dem Himmel meines Lebens*», "Ignorant I confront the heaven of my life"

Written in Paris in early 1913. One of the fragments revised by Rainer Maria Rilke in the *Duino Elegies* period of February, 1922.

Christi Höllenfahrt, Christ's Descent into Hell

Written in Paris in April, 1913.
Rainer Maria Rilke's poetic notion of void and death chimes with Eastern mysticism – with Chuang-tzu, for example, the very wonderful philosopher of ancient China who said 'leap into the boundless and make it your home' (in Willard Johnson: *Riding the Ox Home*, Rider, 1982). This is the thrust of Rilke's poems. The void, which's all absence, flips over in the radiance to become all presence. This overturn is found in mediæval mysticism, such as that of Meister Eckhart, a mystic of *via negativa* (a philosophic stance which chimes with Rilke's Orphic thoughts). Eckhart

described the Godhead in terms of nothingness and blackness, just as in the mediæval mysticism of *The Cloud of Unknowing*, Jan van Ruysbroeck, St John of the Cross and Richard Rolle. Eckhart spoke of descending down 'from nothingness to nothingness', which's another way of describing the Orphic descent of the artist, who descends into the unconscious/ underworld like Orpheus, Isis and Jesus. Poets and mystics such as Dionysius the Areopagite, St John of the Cross, Henry Vaughan and Jan van Ruysbroeck spoke of a radiant darkness, a darkness that was, mysteriously, luminescent, a 'superdazzling darkness' (to use Henry Vaughan's phrase).

In Rainer Maria Rilke's work one finds passages such as these: 'I am open to clear Night's inflowing' (*Poems 1906 to 1926*, 164); night is an erotic space, for in it desires have no visible limits – it is a space where lovers and angels walk, rapt (ib., 110). Night has a pungent feminine flavour in Rilke's work. This corresponds with the interpretation of night in religions and philosophies. For poets, blackness connotes witchcraft, the invisible, blood mysteries, the unknown. Blackness is the space before time, before time and mortality rush to claim the body. Blackness is also Mother Night, the Great Goddess. It is the cosmos itself, the feminine zone of metamorphosis and regeneration. Night becomes womb. Darkness is the seed's space. For the poet, these aspects are linked intuitively: womb = growth = seeds = life = blossoming = love = magic = art = life = death = darkness = womb. These intuitive associations, of mother with night, blackness with occultism, the cosmos with the Great Mother, are found in Rilke's poetry and in many poets. The poet writes of the links between the secret, dark, inner womb-space of the night with the bright, public, everyday, outer world. The poem creates the bridge between inner and outer, dark and light, self and body, private and public.

Wendung, Turning-Point

Written on June 20, 1914, in Paris. Rudolf Kassner (1873-1959), who wrote the epigraph, was an Austrian writer friend. Rainer Maria Rilke wrote to Lou Andreas-Salomé that he had a remarkable poem, written this morning... which I instinctively entitled "Turning-point", because it portrays the turn which must come if I am to live and you will understand what it signifies' (*Briefewechsel   Rainer Maria Rilke and Lou Andreas-Salomé*, 329)

Rilke told Magda von Hattingberg that Kassner's insight had pierced him like a knife. The sacrifice needed, Rilke told Magda, was 'nothing else than a man's unrestricted, never more restrictable resolve to achieve his purest inner possibility' (*Briefwechsel mit Benvenuta*, 97). The quotation from Kassner was in fact a misquotation: Kassner had written 'he who would pass from intensity to greatness must sacrifice himself', but Rilke used it as: 'the way from intensity to greatness leads through sacrifice'. Kassner had noted down the thought during a conversation in Paris with Rilke. It appeared in Kassner's *Sayings of the Yogi* in the *Neue Rundschau* (of 1911), which Rilke had read in Cairo. Later, Rilke told Kassner he had still not achieved 'that turn which my life will have to make in order to be productive of, or even good for anything new' (*Ausgewählte Briefe*, I, 309).

Klage, Complaint

Written in Paris in July, 1914, about ten days after 'Turning-Point'. The angels of the *Duino Elegies* appear here.

An Hölderlin, To Hölderlin

Written in Irschenhausen in September, 1914. Rainer Maria Rilke was greatly impressed by Friedrich Hölderlin (1770-1843), who isn't?, he's one of the great poets of any era. Rilke said he had been reading the first scholarly edition of Hölderlin's poems with

extraordinary feeling and devotion. His influence upon me is great and generous, as only the influence of the richest and inwardly mightiest can be... I cannot tell you how deeply these poems are affecting me and with what inexpressible clarity they stand before me. (letter to Norbert von Hellingrath, July 24, 1914, in Rilke, 1987, 314.

Hellingrath's was the first scholarly edition of Hölderlin's poems, a privately printed volume, which contained many texts previously unpublished. As J.B. Leishman noted, Rilke's discovery of Hölderlin came at a crucial time, soon after the crisis of 'Turning-Point'.

«Nicht daß uns, da wir (plötzlich) erwachsen sind», "Not that, when (suddenly) we are grown-up"

Written in Vienna in early 1916.
1. This phrase was cancelled, but no alternative was added.
2. This stanza was cancelled.

An die Musik, To Music

Written in Munich in 11-12, January, 1918, after a private music concert given by Frau Hanna Wolff.

Gegen-Strophen, Antistrophes

The first few lines of 'Antistrophes' were written in Summer, 1912, in Venice. The rest was written on February 9, 1922, during the bountiful period of creativity at Muzot of the completion of the *Duino Elegies*. 'Antistrophes' was going to be part of the 'Fifth Elegy', but was replaced by the 'Saltimbanques' Elegy. Rainer Maria Rilke spoke of this time as one of 'sacred, elemental disorder', a 'radiant after-storm' of creative activity (in D. Prater, 349).

Sonette II, 4, from Sonette an Orpheus, Sonnet II, 4, *from Sonnets To Orpheus*

Written between 15 and 17, February, 1922. This sonnet uses the unicorn as its central image. Rainer Maria Rilke was fond of mediæval themes and imagery, especially in his early poetry. Rilke wrote a number of poems about the Virgin Mary: the *Life of Mary* is the obvious example: this cycle of poems mirrored the mediæval *Book of Hours*, and was part of Rilke's longlasting love of mediæval and Renaissance religious texts: *The Book of Hours, The Book of Images, The Life of Mary*, and so on.

The unicorn was a powerful symbol related to the Virgin Mary as an image of virginity, purity and innocence in the enclosed garden of mediæval art (such as in the *La Dame à la Licorne* tapestries in the Musée Cluny in Paris). In a letter to Countess Margot Sizzo-Noris-Crouy of June 1, 1923, Rilke explained that the use of the unicorn motif in sonnet II, 4 was not Christian:

> all love of the non-proven, the non-graspable, all belief in the value and reality of whatever our heart has through the centuries created and lifted up out of itself: this is what is praised in this creature. (In Rilke, 1987, 338)

Mausoleum, Mausoleum

Written in October, 1924, in Muzot. An earlier draft was published in *Poems 1906-1926* (331).

«*Nacht. Oh du in Tiefe gelöstes*», "Night. O face against my face"

Written on 2 and 3 October, 1924. The second of the 'The Three Poems', part of the *Night* sequence (unfinished). Rainer Maria Rilke, in his *Duino Elegies,* wrote lyrically of the erotic night that whirls about humans and is full of angels: 'oh, the nights – those nights when the infinite wind eats at our faces!' (*Duino Elegies*, tr. S. Cohn, 21).

Schwerkraft, Gravity

The third of the 'The Three Poems'. Written in Muzot, October 5, 1924.

«*Von nahendem Regen fast zärtlich verdunkelter Garten*», "Garden, tenderly darkened, almost, by nearness of rain or thunder"

Written in Vevey, May 22, 1926. In sonnet II of *Sonnets To Orpheus*, 21 the Rilke-poet bids his heart to sing the praises of 'clear unattainable gardens', the gardens of Shiraz and Ispahan, their water roses, and their ripening figs, so that

> Daß du mit ihren, zwischen den blühenden Zweigen
> wie zum Gesicht gesteigerten Lüften verkehrst...
> (That you are one with their air, the fervid bloom, the breeze between branches, each visionary bough... [tr. L. Norris & A. Keele, 48])

Ankunft, Arrival

Written in Muzot on June 9, 1926.

«*Komm du, du letzter, den ich anerkenne*», "Now come, the last that I can recognize"

Written in mid-December, 1926, Val-Mont. According to J.B. Leishman, this was the last entry in Rainer Maria Rilke's last notebook (*Poems 1906-1926*, 354), and one of his last poems. It characteris about his fatal illness.

«*Rose, oh reiner Widerspruch, Lust*», "Rose, pure contradiction, delight"

Rainer Maria Rilke stipulated in his will of October 27, 1925, that the lines should be carved on his gravestone, with his coat of arms. Rilke wrote of his dislike of the Christian church inter-ferring with death:

> In case I should be overtaken by a grave illness and finally lose full control of my mental faculties, I beg, indeed *implore* my friends to ensure that any priestly support which might press itself forward is kept away from me. Bad enough that I had to admit the doctor as negotiator and middleman in the bodily distress of my nature; any clerical go-between would be an insult and an impediment to the movement of my soul towards the Open. (*Briefe an Nanny Wunderly*, 192)

'Song Is Being'

A Note on Rainer Maria Rilke

by Jeremy Mark Robinson

Rainer Maria Rilke, born René Karl Wilhelm Johann Josef Maria Rilke in Prague on December 4, 1875, is one of the greatest of all lyrical poets.[1] Rainer Maria Rilke is part of that group of modern European poets and writers which includes Guillaume Apollinaire, Friedrich Nietzsche, Arthur Rimbaud, Georg Trakl, Marina Tsvetayeva, Marcel Proust, Stéphane Mallarmé, W.B. Yeats, Thomas Mann, Paul Claudel, Laforgue, Stefen George, and friends such as André Gide, Lou Andreas-Salomé and Paul Valéry. Rilke mixed, in Munich in the Great War years, with people like the astronomer Erwein von Aretin, the artist Paul Klee, the poet Hans Carossa, the art historian Wilhelm Hausenstein and the dancer Clotilde von Derp. Rainer Maria Rilke's world is that of *mittel* Europe, German-speaking Czechoslovakia, Austria and Germany, and cities of the late 19th century and early 20th century: Vienna, Prague, Munich, Berlin, Paris. Although he moved towards the culture of French writers such as

Valéry and Gide towards the end of his life, the world Rilke comes out of is the Germanic one of Franz Kafka, Egon Schiele, Ludwig Wittgenstein, Paul Celan, Karl Kraus, Robert Musil and Trakl. Although he disliked being categorized as a German artist, Rilke is clearly from the Germanic tradition: in philosophy, the transcendent ethics and dialectics of Immaneuel Kant and Georg Wilhelm Friedrich Hegel, the pessimism and mysticism of Arthur Schopenhauer, the tragic Hellenism of Friedrich Nietzsche, the lyrical effusion of Johann Wolfgang von Goethe, Friedrich Schiller, Ludwig von Kleist, Heinrich Heine and Novalis.

The fervent Hellenism of Friedrich Hölderlin and the magic idealism of Novalis seem particularly aligned with Rainer Maria Rilke's poetic sensibilities, even if he were not directly influenced by them (he certainly was by Hölderlin). Rilke's life appeared to be one of restlessness and rootlessness: he spent the life, it seems, of the archetypal romantic, introspective, bourgeois European outsider. The outsider figure crops up in the works of J.-K. Huysmans, Jean-Paul Sartre, André Gide, Knut Hamsun, Fyodor Dostoievsky, D.H. Lawrence, Thomas Mann, Herrmann Hesse, E.M. Forster and others.

Rainer Maria Rilke's life fascinates critics, and it's easy to see why: his life embodies a certain kind of highly cultured, post-imperial European heritage. There are the extraordinary number of friendships with (often older) women, such as Princess Marie von Thurm und Taxis, Lou Andreas-Salomé, Nanny Wunderly (Rilke called her 'Nîke'), Elizabeth Dorothee Klossowska ('Merline'), Magda von Hattingberg ('Benvenuta'), Eva Cassirer, Paula Modersohn-Becker, Hertha Koenig, Sidonie Nádherny von Borutin ('Sidie'), Regina Ullmann, Adelmina Romanelli ('Mimi'), Marianne Weininger ('Mieze'), Agapia Valmarana ('Pia'), Mathilde Vollmoeller, Theodora von der Müness ('Dory'); the list goes on.

There are the key meetings with European artists (Auguste Rodin, Stefan George, André Gide, Paul Valéry); the ætherealized romances; the ever-changing philosophy; the endless letters; his mysterious, inward-looking personality; and the way in which his art and his life seem to be intimately intertwined. All these aspects of Rainer Maria Rilke, among others, make him such a intriguing object for biographical or critical investigation. Also, not forgetting, his incredible poetry.

Rainer Maria Rilke is one of those artists who is eulogized as a saint, a martyr, a mystic, a prophet of his age. Like writers such as Johann Wolfgang von Goethe, William Shakespeare and Miguel de Cervantes, Rilke is thought to have something profound to say about life. However, Rilke did not not resolve the many conflicts in his life, just as Dante Alighieri or André Gide didn't: Rilke remained in a state of ontological flux and ambivalence to the end of his life. He was an acutely sensitive individual – particularly to people and places. He was seldom satisfied with any particular place, though, and often yearned for some other place. Even though he holed up in some of Europe's finest locations, he would pine for somewhere else. In this he recalls the archetypal traveller, the drifter, who must always have a departure date in mind. No permanency for Rilke, but a residence in a place which must always have the hope at the end of it of moving on somewhere else.

Rainer Maria Rilke was exquisitely sensitive to æsthetics – to flowers, for example (he wrote many poems about roses), to furnishings (he loved to have a standing desk at which to work), to food and architecture. Elizabeth Sewell wrote that Rilke 'was from the beginning a hypersensitive being and apparently without the robust stamina a poet needs'.[2] However, Rilke's life reveals that he was at times ruthlessly determined to follow his poetic calling. Seemingly wan and weak from the outside (he was discharged from active military service on health grounds), he was also ambitious and self-determined.

Many of Rainer Maria Rilke's relationships were idealized, non-sexual interweavings, often occurring over long distances, by letter. He maintained a number of relationships with what were really muses. The litany of Rilkean muses include Merline, Magda, Andreas-Salomé, Sidie, Clara, Loulou, Nîke and the Princess Marie. There were heroines, too, for Rilke, such as the Virgin Mary, Eurydice, Mary Magdalene and Alcestis. Few major poets have had so many women friends, so many potential muses and so many of them reciprocated with advice, help, money, places to stay. They listened to him reading poetry (weeping at the right moments), they begged to stay with him, begged him to stay with them, gave him money and love. Rilke was one of the most feminized of poets, but he also was deeply ambivalent in his attitudes towards women. He feared and desired them, alternately yearning for intimacy, then retreating to a safe distance.

Rainer Maria Rilke said he had searched for some kind of ecstatic connection with women but had failed to find it. He told Salomé on October 21, 1913 that it seemed as if he were always 'standing at the telescope, ascribing to every approaching woman a bliss which was certainly never to be found with any one of them: my own bliss, the bliss I once found in my most solitary hours'.[3]

Rainer Maria Rilke's love affairs were marked by the familiar patterns of fascination and flight, of drawing near to the beloved and an escape back into the self. Rilke seemed fated never to find an enduring erotic relationship. Yet, as Princess Marie commented, Rilke 'cannot live without the atmosphere of a woman around him'.[4] Maybe Rilke was unwilling or even incapable of committing himself to one person for decades. Princess Marie told Hugo von Hofmannstahl that Rilke was 'incapable of feeling either friendship or love, and *knew it*, and suffered endlessly thereby'.[5]

Rainer Maria Rilke was an incredibly inventive creator of poetry, who could forge the myriad states and images of love, from the delicate, detailed and subtle, to the passionate, illuminating and ecstatic. Rilke was adept at inflecting language with blissful emotions. But while he could describe the many experiences of love, he found it difficult to turn them into realities, to act on his words. For Rilke, love could be a transitory, fragile state between two people. 'Why do people who love each other separate before there is any need? Because it is after all so very temporary a thing, to be together and to love one another'. Rilke saw life as a 'continuous flow of vicissitudes', change following change, so that parting was inevitable, and people should become used to it ('at any moment be ready to give each other up, let be and not hold each other back'.[6]

Rainer Maria Rilke gives the impression of being a childless, bachelor type, quietly going about his life of sublime interiority and brilliant poetry. The sense of being childless accords so well with one's impressions of poets such as Thomas Hardy, Novalis, D.H. Lawrence and Arthur Rimbaud. Yet it is surprising to realize that Rilke did have children – as did Dante Alighieri, Francesco Petrarch, André Gide and John Cowper Powys. In Rilke's case, he had a child early on. But there is no sense that Rilke would become the stereotypical 'family man'. Magda von Hattingberg, one of Rilke's many women admirers, could not believe that Rilke was married with children. Indeed, this fact was one of the reasons she did not become a long-term lover in the traditional, heterosexual, bourgeois sense.

Much of his life was spent in exile from his family. 'My family is not a home, and is not to be one', Rilke wrote to Gustaf af Geijerstam on February 7th, 1907.[7] This is surprising, perhaps, seen from the outside. For clearly Rilke was a highly emotional man who seemed to crave affection, discussion, *contact* with other people. Surprising, then, to find his attitude to his wife Clara and his child so apparently off-hand and distanced. The needs of the artist in him consistently triumphed. Rilke, though a father early on, kept escaping from the family situation, to lead a restless bachelor life. One biographer claims that if Rilke had stayed in his marriage with Clara Westoff he 'could never have found himself' (D. Prater, 85). Rilke said he wanted Clara to 'reach the greatest heights as an artist', in order that she might succeed artistically, he left her, 'not to disturb her and turn her into a "housewife"'.[8] In a letter to his wife, of September 5, 1902, Rilke said that one must choose life or art: '[e]ither happiness of art'. Artists such as Leo Tolstoy and Auguste Rodin, Rilke said to Clara, let their lives go to ruin, while their work thrived.

Rainer Maria Rilke found patrons, many of them, throughout his life. People seemed to want to help the intellectual poet. People gave him money, offered him accommodation, helped Rilke out when he was in trouble. The list of people who helped him is long, including Anton Kippenberg, his publisher at Insel-Verlag, and also many female admirers: Eva Cassirer, Princess Marie, Magda Richling, Lou Andreas-Salomé, Clara Westoff and Sidonie Nádherny.

❧

Lou Andreas-Salomé (1861-1937), one of the key women in Rainer Maria Rilke's life, was an extraordinary personality, by any standards. Of course, much of her glamour derives from her associations with three great European minds: Friedrich Nietzsche, Sigmund Freud and Rilke. However, she was a talented writer and psychoanalyst in her own right, as demonstrated by her novels (*Ruth, Fenitschka, Ma*), her short stories (*Im Zwischenland*), studies of Rilke and Nietzsche (*Rainer Maria Rilke*, 1929, *Friedrich Nietzsche in seinen Werken*, 1894), and her psychoanalytic texts. Rilke had been interested in Nietzsche's philosophy before he met Salomé: not only had Nietzsche stated God was dead, he also said that art's goal was God-making.[9]

Friedrich Nietzsche, Rainer Maria Rilke and Sigmund Freud – it's an incredible trio of minds, and Lou Andreas-Salomé knew them well. She was born Louise von Salomé in 1861, in St Petersburg, of a Russian general and a German mother. She studied philosophy and theology at Zurich university (she was one of the first female students). She had an infamous affair with both Paul Rée and Nietzsche, and married Friedrich Carl Andreas in 1887.

Paul Rée and Friedrich Nietzsche would take long walks with Lou Andreas-Salomé, discussing philosophy. The men in their thirties were deeply enamoured of Andreas-Salomé, and it appears that she was largely in control of the love triangle. Nietzsche made the mistake of asking Rée to convey his proposal of marriage to Andreas-Salomé.

Lou Andreas-Salomé was an inspiring woman, quite brilliant, who ignited Rilke poetically as well as sexually. She also knew Hans Hofmannsthal, Arthur Schnitzler, Jakob Wassermann, Richard Wagner, Count Eduard Keyserling, Joseph Conrad, Franz Wedekind, Leo Tolstoy, Ivan Turgenev and Georg Brandes. 'Europe's cultural élite paid homage to Lou Salomé', wrote H.F. Peters.[10] Friedrich Nietzsche was besotted with her, calling her 'sharp-sighted as an eagle and courageous as a lion'.[11] For Sigmund Freud, Andreas-Salomé was someone who displayed 'all the peaceful and playful charm of true egoism'. Andreas-Salomé's beauty led Freud to compare her to a cat.[12] Salomé took Rilke in 1913 to a Psychoanalytic Congress, and introduced him to Freud.

Lou Andreas-Salomé was the only erotic/ philosophic focus in

Nietzsche's otherwise celibate experience of women.[13] Her refusal of him, so legend had it, led to his insanity. In a letter to Henry Miller, Lawrence Durrell wrote:

Anaïs [Nin] just sent me a biography of Lou [Andreas-Salomé] by [H.F.] Peters which is marvellous, it was Lou who started off this whole thing in Geneva – her wicked sexy spirit – the spirit of the Great Instigators, like that of Anaïs herself![14]

In the novel *Livia*, Lawrence Durrell depicted Andreas-Salomé as 'a dramatic and beautiful Slav whose extravagant and fleshy *ampleur* was somehow wholly sexy and composed'.[15] French feminist Sarah Kofman has wondered whether Lou Andreas-Salomé was a model for that narcissistic woman which men love, the type that demands to be loved. Kofman considers this narcissistic woman in relation to Nietzsche, and wonders whether Andreas-Salomé was the mediator of the theory of narcissism between Nietzsche and Freud.[16] Andreas-Salomé's notion of the narcissistic woman, and her thoughts on the artist, influenced Nietzsche.

She was an independent thinker, quite the equal of any of the intellectual minds with which she came into contact. 'She was strikingly beautiful,' writes Rilke's biographer, Donald Prater,

although thoroughly 'liberated' in ideas and scornful of convention, had led a life in which, despite appearances, heterosexual love played no part. (37)

One of Lou Andreas-Salomé's biographers (Rudolph Binion) was not so convinced by her liberal views. He saw her as suffering from an infantile father complex, which manifested itself in her relation to Freud in her mid-life. According to Binion, Andreas-Salomé exhibited penis envy, felt inferior to men and apparently even wished to 'make herself master' over Freud (240-1, 349, 354, 397).

The Rainer Maria Rilke-Andreas-Salomé romance appeared to be spiritual, idealistic, Platonic – Rainer Rilke and Lou Andreas-Salomé went about Russia hand in hand. They were, Andreas-Salomé said later, 'like brother and sister, but from primeval times before incest became a sacrilege';[17] they were, she said, a Neoplatonic unity: 'body and soul indivisibly one' (ib., 9). For Andreas-Salomé, she achieved with Rilke a 'kneeling-together', not sex but a supra-sexual sacrament, a holy love. His experience of her was bound up with his time in Russia, his child-like notions of motherhood, his love of the Madonnas of Italian Renaissance painting, and his creative hunger.

❧

Rainer Maria Rilke's early poetry includes work such as *Leben und Lieder* (1894), *Traumgekrönt* (1897), the novel *The Notebooks of Malte Laurids Brigge*, *Advent* (1897), and *Buch der Bilder* (*The Book of Pictures*), *The Book of Hours* and *Cornet* (1899). These are the books of the early period, which is usually dated from the middle 1890s to the time of the breakthrough *New Poems* (1906). Rilke's early poetry is often mannered, precious, derivative, trite, banal and self-conscious. Like Stéphane Mallarmé and Paul Valéry – with Georg Trakl the poets whom he resembles in many ways – Rilke was a precise poet, who dreamt of the perfect form for the perfect poetic expression. Few poets are as exact as Rilke. It is partly this poetic brilliance that makes him so highly regarded. 'Rarely has a European poet stirred so many minds and inspired so many pens', wrote F.W. von Heerikhuizen. As Frank Wood put it, '[t]he craft aspect of his work, the creativity of the "word", is the very key to his æsthetic, thought, and "message"' (218).

Rainer Maria Rilke was not a vague, dithering personality, as his sometimes wispy poetry might indicate. He was though short in stature a solid, very sensual character. He wasn't a wispy character, said the artist Hermann Burte, but rational, orderly and down-to-earth.[18] He actually enjoyed the whole craft of writing, the very physicality of it. One must love not only the work itself, but 'also the manual labour that goes with it', Rilke said.[19] Rilke enshrined the act of writing itself – not only the cerebral and emotional pleasure of putting words together, but also the feel of the pen scratching over the surface of the paper. This love of writing by hand in itself is shown by the abundance of letters he wrote. He was fastidious too about the physical quality of his books. Working on the publication of *The Book of Images*, Rilke was much concerned with the binding, paper and type. He wanted even the smallest word to be 'like a monument'. Every word must be printed exactly right.[20]

Much of Rainer Maria Rilke's life centred around his desk, working at a table, or his favoured standing desk. For hours and days on end, Rilke, like most writers, would have sat at his desk and worked. One of the primary tasks he did was to write a huge amount of letters. He is one of literature's great letter-writers. He would conduct love affairs through the post (as with Magda von Hattingberg). He worked, day by day, on projects such as translating Dante Alighieri's *Vita Nuova*, André Gide and Elizabeth Barrett Browning's *Sonnets from the Portuguese*; essays such as "On the Young Poet", "Primal Sound" and "Some Reflections on Dolls"; *The Rodin-Book*; and of course poems. Among other projects he considered were translations from Francesco Petrarch and St Augustine's *Confessions*; a pæan for the dancer Vaslav Nijinsky. Then there was his reading – his love of poets such as Heinrich von Kleist, Paul Claudel, Friedrich Hölderlin and Franz Werfel – Gide, Early Renaissance painters, Auguste Rodin.

Rainer Maria Rilke's poetry is marked by passion, distance, synæthesia, ambivalence, openness, and formal elegance. Though his stanza forms, for example, are meticulously organized, he is describing often violent and disturbing states of consciousness, which slip into prophetic magic on the one hand, and anguish on the other. In his poems Rilke asks questions such as 'have you ever *really* looked at a bowl of roses before?', questions which poets have been asking since the birth of poetry. Rilke shows these things – an iris, panther, a statue of Apollo – as if they were new. Rilke's technique of synæsthesia makes him as much a tactile poet or an aural poet as a visual poet. Synæsthesia is one of the poet's goals, Rilke says in his short essay "Primal Sound". Too many modern poems employ only one or two of the five senses, Rilke says in *The Rodin-Book* (130). In *The Sonnets To Orpheus* (I, 14) he speaks of the rainbow of the senses, and the language of flowers and fruits. In sonnet I, 16 he asks 'who can point a finger at a smell?'. He often spoke of the soundscape or aural geography of places – the way a spring would be quiet though it was flowing speedily, or the way the roaring of a river might carve out the walls of a valley. 'Reine Spannung. O Musik der Kräfte!' he wrote in the twelfth *Sonnet To Orpheus* ('electric tension. Music of energy!')[21] Rilke's acute sensitivity to sound is obvious in his heavily musical verse, but also in his fastidiousness about his living quarters. He longed for peace, and at times loathed the prospect of small talk.

Rainer Maria Rilke's poetic world, with its dark spaces in which haunted sounds echo, recalls the dark worlds of touch that occur in stories of blindness (such as D.H. Lawrence's *The Blind Man*). It is a world of the sixth sense, the magical sense, the 'supersense', the occult faculties that everyone possesses but which society suppresses. Like most great poets, Rilke is a supremely synæsthetic poet, speaking to all of the senses, and the sixth, præternatural sense. The link here, historically, is Symbolism, with its emphasis (in poets such as Paul Verlaine and Stéphane Mallarmé), on the musicality, materiality and 'thingness' of poetry. In his essay "Primal Sound" Rilke voiced the common claim that modern European art over-emphasizes the visual sense while neglecting the others.

Rainer Maria Rilke's technique, in emphasizing the materiality of the word, which goes far beyond T.S. Eliot and Ezra Pound, is to work from within. In Rilkean poetics, poetic language must be made rich and full, but without being over-indulgent or pretentious. A poem enters into language from within,' Rilke wrote,

> in an aspect forever averted from us. It fills the language wondrously, rising to its very brim – but it never again thrusts towards us.[22]

The best poets create this sense of fullness, like a glass of water filled up to the brim, the meniscus poised to break, balanced on the point of flooding. Rainer Maria Rilke's poems operate at this balancing point between openness and closure, between centripedal and centrifugal motion, the poem being all symbol and being all object. Rilke developed the inwardness of poetry begun in the poetry of Charles Baudelaire and refined in Stéphane Mallarmé into new depths of self-referentiality. *Verinnerlichung* was the term for this transmutation from outer to inner, while instead of 'work of art' Rilke used the term *Kunstding* ('thing of art'). There is conflict between the 'in-seeing' of the

Neue Gedichte period and the Orphic philosophy of the late works. The fundamental innerness remains consistent.

❧

Rainer Maria Rilke was a cosmopolitan poet, at home in many different places but still forever in search of his 'spiritual home'. Indeed, one of the main Rilke critics, Eudo C. Mason, said that Rilke 'gives the impression of being one of the completely culturally cosmopolitan beings that has ever existed' (1963, 2). There was no single place in Rilke's cosmology that was the mythic centre – as Dorset was for Thomas Hardy, or Paris for Gertrude Stein. Rilke's is a poetry not so much of exile and displacement, like so much of post-18th century poetry, as people migrated *en masse*; rather, Rilke's is a poetry of no particular place (even though it is distinctly made in Europe, with a slant now termed white Eurocentric). Rilke does not, for example, exalt particular places, or write eulogies to particular landscapes. There are references in his work to sites such as the Luxembourg Gardens in Paris, or the Tuscan countryside. But Rilke is not a 'landscape' poet, a 'nature' poet in the traditional sense. He is not provincial, nor slangy or colloquial. His poetry is, rather, deliberately Orphic, purely lyrical, a poetry of everyplace, everytime.

After the struggle of the *Duino Elegies* comes the relative calm of the *Sonnets To Orpheus* (in fact, most of the *Sonnets* were written before the *Elegies* were completed). The conventional view is that Rainer Maria Rilke struggled for years between the beginning and completion of the *Duino Elegies,* hardly writing anything in between. In fact, he was working for much of that time, and had creative periods as rich (or nearly as rich) as that of February, 1922. Rilke had many beginnings throughout that time. In 1914 he wrote to Sidie Nadherny:

> I'm stuck in the pressure of the new beginning, which I want to do *well, well* (it can easily be ruined), what I want is a pure spiritual life, every day the same, no distractions, no claims on me, *all expectation turned inward* toward the heart where my next task must emerge.

This is typical of Rainer Maria Rilke, aching for the space and time to be free of familial, societal and financial responsibilities, to concentrate on a new beginning. Each phase of work, even each work, can be seen as a new beginning for artists. This is Rilke's eternal problem: to prepare the space in which the new beginning can blossom. 'What's needed is just this: loneliness, vast inner loneliness', he wrote in 1903.[23]

The breakthrough of the *Sonnets To Orpheus* and the *Duino Elegies*, when it came, in 1922, was quite extraordinary. Rainer Maria Rilke was staying at the Château de Muzot near Sierre in Switzerland, on the River Rhône. The poet had been waiting for years for this moment – a decade, in fact. He seems to have spent years moving about Europe listlessly – never satisfied, never attaining the peace he desired to write the poems he knew were inside him. He seems to have spent years searching for the right balance of space, place, time and friendship. In short, a quest for a creative solitude in which to nurture the poems he knew were gestating inside him. Before the creative floodgates opened in a truly dramatic style at Muzot in 1922, Rilke seems to have spent years in the wilderness, in a creative pregnancy.

The poet, Julia Kristeva suggests, writes inside the mother, in a sense, or from the mother, or from the maternal realm. 'The poet's *jouissance* that causes him to emerge from schizophrenic decorporealization is the *jouissance* of the mother', comments Kristeva.[24] Rilke's burst into creative work was just such a birth from the maternal realm. But what a gestation! A decade of it. The glory is that, not only did he complete the *Duino Elegies* in this outpouring, but also wrote the sublime *Sonnets To Orpheus*, clearly his crowning achievement. Up until this moment in February, 1922 one sees Rilke moving from place to place, first Paris, then Munich, then Italy, back and forth across Europe, always pining for utter solitude, and only attaining it for all too brief moments. One might have thought he would never write anything great again – nothing approaching the best of the *New Poems*, for example. One view might have seen Rilke as written out, a poet who had written some marvellous lyrics in his youth, but who appeared to be creatively exhausted. Certainly the rituals of letter-writing which he indulged in did not seem to work as well as he hoped. For years, it seems, when he had found his solitude-space – the Paris apartment, for example, or the rooms in Munich – he would start writing letters, to clear his desk. This was his ritual prelude to the real work – that is, writing poetry. But it didn't work. For ages the creative lift-off didn't happen. When it finally did, the poet seemed to be as amazed as his admirers. The creative forces flowed through him: Friedrich Hölderlin had spoken of being 'struck by Apollo', a violent image of inspiration. It was similarly tumultuous for Rilke. To gauge the significance of the outpouring of poetry, one only has to look at a couple of the *Sonnets To Orpheus*. They are absolutely supreme.

For Rainer Maria Rilke, it was an astonishment that the poetry came so suddenly – and also that his friends had been so patient with him. He thanked Anton Kippenberg profusely: 'that *you* have made this possible for me, been so patient with me: *ten* years! Thanks!' (ib.) It was a victory, he wrote to Nîke, 'Victory! Victory!'25 The creative juices were still flowing four days after the completion of the first cycle of the *Sonnets To Orpheus,* when, on February 11, 1922, Rilke rewrote most of the 'Tenth Elegy'. On February 13 another sonnet was composed; the next day, the 'Saltimbanques' Elegy was written. This replaced the 'Antistrophes' poem (included here), becoming the 'Fifth Elegy'.

Rainer Maria Rilke spoke of this time as one of 'sacred, elemental disorder', a 'radiant after-storm'. The final creative outburst was the completion in nine days of the second cycle of the *Sonnets To Orpheus*. 'The only thing we really own,' Rilke wrote to Nîke, 'is patience, but what a capital that represents – and what interest it bears, in due time!' Rilke maintained that he was as surprised by the arrival of the *Sonnets* as anyone: they 'are perhaps the most mysterious, most enigmatic dictation I have ever endured and achieved.'26 Like poets of old, Rilke was thankful to the gods, the muses, or whoever presided over creativity – grateful that he had lived long enough to be able to complete this major work:

> Just think! I have been allowed to survive to this point. Through everything. Miracle. Grace... Now I know myself again. My heart was as though truncated while the Elegies were not done. Now they are. They exist.

Here is magic; existence is magical; being here is glorious; these are examples of Rainer Maria Rilke's total affirmation of life. These are not the outpourings of a madman spouting off in a crazed Nietzschean manner, but primary poetic assertions of the magic of life. The question is, why isn't life magical all the time?

All you have to do in life is to be. Be what, exactly? Just *be*, says Rainer Maria Rilke: 'all we basically have to do is to *be*, but simply, earnestly, the way the earth simply is', he wrote in *Letters On Cézanne*.

> Gesang ist Dasein. Für ein Gott ein Leichtes.
> Wann aber *sind* wir?

the poet asked in the *Sonnets To Orpheus* ('Song is Being. It's easy for a god. But when shall we *be*?' I, 3. 7-8, 3). To simply *be* is really difficult, as Novalis and Rilke admit. Yet it is the goal. To realize, as the Hindu mystics put it, that Thou Art That (*tat tvam asi*). The point is, Rilke said in a letter, 'to live everything. *Live* the questions now'.[27] Rilke's transformations are psychological. All his energies are concentrated inwards. Sonnet I, 22 of the *Sonnets To Orpheus* is about timelessness:

> denn das Verweilende
> erst weiht uns ein

he writes ('only the timeless begins us and lights us', 22).

With the *Duino Elegies* and the *New Poems*, the *Sonnets To Orpheus* are Rainer Maria Rilke's greatest poetic achievement. Each poet invents poetic forms anew, and Rilke reclaims the sonnet from its traditional use as a short lyric, usually treating experiences associated with love. Rilke's sonnets have little to do with the great European sonnet tradition – of Dante Alighieri, Francesco Petrarch, William Shakespeare and the Elizabethans. Remember, though, that Rilke had translated Elizabeth Barrett Browning's *Sonnets From the Portuguese*. Charles Baudelaire is probably another reference point, in his modernization of the sonnet. Rilke takes the sonnet form and, like Petrarch, bends it into all sorts of shapes. He will, like Shakespeare, construct a sonnet from a single sentence, with many clauses and intervals. Or he will, like Baudelaire, create a series of short, punchy phrases which break up each line. Rilke's sonnets do not follow but modulate the old rules of the octave and sestet. Rilke does usually stick to one important tradition in the sonnet, the rhyme (which's partly why he is so difficult to translate). Rilke packs a lot into the fourteen-line space of the sonnet. He evokes night, space, breath, presence, transformation, loss, suffering, sensuality (sound: ringing like a bell, taste: wine, sight: night, and so on), mystery, magic, personification (earth, water, wine, night), philosophy.

While other poets have a 'landscape of the soul', some space that is their own creation and refers to some part of the planet – a town, a country, a house (Greece for Friedrich Hölderlin, Lord Byron and Lawrence Durrell, Paris and New York for Henry Miller, the Vaucluse for Petrarch, Florence for Dante, Alexandria for C.P. Cavafy), the Rilke-poet's soul-space is abstract. Rilke's inner landscapes hardly fuse with the everyday outer world at all. The dark inner soul-spaces accord, rather, with the abstractions of art. With Islamic abstract art, with the spatial mysticism of Renaissance masters such as Piero della Francesca (all those pastel-hued planes of mystery), with the timeless, flat friezes of ancient Egypt and Rome, or the quiet intensity of Dutch still-life painting. Rilke's sense of space is internalized. It is essential, Rilke said, to use the 'generous spaces, these spaces of *ours*', inside us ('Seventh Elegy'). Rainer Maria Rilke's sense of space goes beyond the metaphysics of Symbolism and beyond the symbol itself (see sonnet I, 11). In poems such as 'Archäischer Torso Apollos' one sees the post-Symbolist sense of space emerging. The new sense of space derives partially from Auguste Rodin's and Rilke's re-appraisal of sculpture. Statues fascinated Rilke. In a fragment of an elegy he spoke of 'der Statuen ewiges Dastehn' (the 'infinite thereness of statues').[28] Of ancient statues, Rilke wrote (to Lou Andeas-Salomé on August 15, 1903), that no one knows who made them, no personal history 'casts a shadow over their naked clarity: they *are*. That is all' (ib., 303). Some of Rodin's sculptures, Rilke said, had a similar quality. Like the dancer, the sculpture actualizes space around it. Inside becomes all outside. The dancer becomes, wildly, the space s/he moves within; the sculpture, too, sets alive the space surrounding it. The statue in 'Archaic Torso of

Apollo' actually comes alive.

In 20th century poetry, symbolism leads in a multitude of directions – in Rainer Maria Rilke's case, to 'the Open'. While Rilke's 'Open' doesn't have the same authority that the Christian God has (or had), it is no less authentic, or meaningful, in the terms of modern art. Sonnet II, 13 is one of the great poems of Rilkean beingness:

> Sei – und wisse zugleich des Nicht-Seins Bedingung,
> den unendlichen Grund deiner innigen Schwingung,
> daß du die völlig vollziehst dieses einzige Mal.
> (Be – and at the same time know Non-Being, the infinite ground for the
> harmonic of your heart, so you sound it perfectly once, and only once.)[29]

Notes

Please also refer to the Bibliography

1. Eudo C. Mason reckons that Rainer Maria Rilke could have been a great novelist, a first rate critic and perhaps also a great dramatist – but his sense of lyrical interiority eventually became dominant (1963, 12).

2. E. Sewell, 1961, 310.

3. Rilke, *Briefwechsel Rainer Maria Rilke und Lou Andreas-Salomé*, 305.

4. Fürstin Marie von Thurn und Taxis-Hohenlohe, 1966, 107.

5. Hofmanstahl, 1929, in *Neue Zürcher Zeitung*, Oct 6, 1982.

6. Rilke, letter to E.S. zu Schweinsberg, November 4, 1909, in *Briefe 1907-1914*, 80-81.

7. Quoted in D. Prater, 141.

8. Quoted in D. Prater, 86.

9. *The Selected Poems of Rainer Maria Rilke*, tr. S. Mitchell, xvii.

10. See A. Livingstone, 1984; H.F. Peters, 1960, 52.

11. F. Nietzsche: *Briefe an Peter Gast*, Leipzig, 1924, 89-90.

12. See S. Freud: "On Narcissism", *Complete Works*, vol. 14, 88f; S. Kofman, 50f; Mary Jacobus: *Reading Woman: essays in feminist criticism*, Methuen, 1986, 135.

13. Janet Lungstrum: "Nietzsche Writing Woman/ Woman Writing Nietzsche", in P.J. Burgard, ed. *Nietzsche and the Feminine*, University Press of Virginia, Charlottesville, 1994, 144.

14. Lawrence Durrell: *The Durrell-Miller Letters 1935-1980*, Faber, 1988, 466.

15. Lawrence Durrell: *Livia*, Faber, 1978, 187.

16. Sarah Kofman, 1985; see also Biddy Martin: *Woman and Modernity: The (Life)Styles of Lou Andreas-Salomé*, Cornell University Press, Ithaca, 1991.

17. Lou Andreas-Salomé: *Lebenstrückblick*, ed. Ernst Pfeiffer, Insel-Taschenbuch, Frankfurt 1974, 138.

18. Quoted in D. Prater, 263.

19. Rilke, letter to Dora Herzheimer, July 14, 1907, in Obermuller, 1966.

20. Rilke, *Briefe an Axel Juncker*, Insel Verlag, Leipzig, 1979, 35.

21. *The Sonnets To Orpheus*, I, 12. 9, in *Sonnets To Orpheus*, tr. Leslie Norris & Alan Keele, 12.

22. *Letters to Benvenuta*, 51.

23. *Duino Elegies*, tr. J.B. Leishman, 120.

24. Julia Kristeva. *The Kristeva Reader*, ed. T. Moi, Blackwell, 1986, 192.

25. *Briefe an Nanny Wunderly-Volkart*, 1977, 668f.

26. Rilke, letter, April 20, 1923, in *The Selected Poems of Rainer Maria Rilke*, tr. S. Mitchell, 336.

27. Rilke, *Rilke On Love and Other Difficulties*, 25.

28. Rilke, in *The Selected Poems of Rainer Maria Rilke*, tr. S. Mitchell, 214-5.

29. *Sonnets To Orpheus*, tr. Leslie Norris & Alan Keele, 40.

Selected Bibliography

RAINER MARIA RILKE

The Book of Images, tr. Edward Snow, North Point Press/ Farrar, Straus & Giroux, New York, 1994

The Book of Hours, tr. Strayer, University of Salzburg Press, 1995

Rodin and Other Prose Pieces, tr. G. Craig Houston, Quartet, 1986

An Unofficial Rilke: Poems 1912-1926, tr. Michael Hamburger, Anvil Press Poetry, 1981

Translations From the Poetry of Rainer Maria Rilke, tr. M.D. Herter Norton, W.W. Norton, 1993

New Poems, tr. J.B. Leishman, Hogarth Press, 1963

Rose Window and Other Verse From New Poems, Bullfinch, 1999

Poems 1906 to 1926, tr. J.B. Leishman, Hogarth Press, 1957

Rilke On Love and Other Difficulties: Translations and Considerations of Rainer Maria Rilke, John J.L. Mood, W.W. Norton, 1993

Requiem and Other Poems, tr. J.B. Leishman, Hogarth Press, 1935

Duino Elegies, tr. J.B. Leishman & Stephen Spender, Hogarth Press, 1957

Duino Elegies, tr. Stephen Cohn, Carcanet Press, 1989

Duino Elegies and the Sonnets To Orpheus, Boston, 1977

Sonnets To Orpheus, tr. J.B. Leishman, Hogarth Press, 1946

Sonnets To Orpheus, tr. Leslie Norris & Alan Keele, Skoob Books, 1991

Sonnets To Orpheus, tr. R. Hunter, Hulogosi Communications, 1993

Later Poems, tr. J.B. Leishman, Hogarth Press, 1938

Selected Poems, tr. J.B. Leishman, Penguin, 1964

The Selected Poetry of Rainer Maria Rilke tr. Stephen Mitchell, Picador, 1987

Selected Poems of Rainer Maria Rilke, tr. Robert Bly, Harper & Row, New York, 1981

Between Roots: Rilke, tr. Rika Lesser, Princeton University Press, New Jersey, 1989

Selected Works, tr. G. Craig Houston & J.B. Leishman, Hogarth Press, 2 vols, 1954/60

The Best of Rilke tr. Walter Arndt, University Press of New England,

Hanover, 1989

Poems, tr. Jessie Lemont, Columbia University Press, New York, 1943

Complete French Poems, tr. A. Paulin, Graywolf, 1987

Ahead of All Parting, Random House, 1997

Poems, tr. J.B. Leishman, Everyman, 1996

Testament, ed. E. Zinn, Frankfurt, 1975

The Notebook of Malte Laurids Brigge, tr. M.D. Hertert Norton, Norton, New York, 1964

Diaries of a Young Poet, tr. E. Snow & M. Winkler, Norton, 1998

Selected Letters, 1902-1926, tr. R.C. Hull, 1946

Letters On Cézanne, ed. Clara Rilke, Cape, 1988

Letters to Benvenuta, tr. Heinz Norden, Hogarth Press, 1953

Letters to a Young Poet, tr. Reginald Snell, Sidgwick & Jackson, 1945

Letters to Merline, 1919-1922, tr. Violet & M. MacDonald, Methuen, 1951

The Letters of Rainer Maria Rilke and Princess Maria von Thurn und Taxis, tr. Nora Wydenbruck, Hogarth Press, 1988

Gesammalte Briefe 1892-1926, Insel Verlag, Leipzig, 3, 1936-39

Briefe aus Muzot, 1921-1926, Insel Verlag, Leipzig, 1935 & 1937

Briefe an Nanny Wunderly-Volkart, Insel Verlag, Leipzig, 1977

Briefe, vol. 1, 1897-1914, vol. 2, 1914-1926, Insel Verlag, Leipzig, 1950

Briefwechsel mit Benvenuta, Esslingen, 3, 1936-39

Briefwechsel Rainer Maria Rilke und Lou Andreas-Salomé, Insel Verlag, 1975

Rainer Maria Rilke/ André Gide, Correspondance, 1909-1926, Paris, 1952

Briefewechsel Rainer Maria Rilke und Marie von Thurn und Taxis, Insel Verlag, Leipzig, 1951

Briefewechsel an Sidonie Nádherny, Insel Verlag, Leipzig, 1973

Correspondance Rilke/ André Gide/ Emile Verhaeren, Paris, 1955

OTHERS

Lou Albert-Lasard. *Wege mit Rilke*, Frankfurt, 1952

Lou Andreas-Salomé. *The Freud Journal*, tr. Stanley A. Leavy, Hogarth Press, 1965

—. *Rainer Maria Rilke*, Leipzig, 1928

—. *Lebensrückblick*, ed. Ernst Pfeiffer, Tachenbuch 54, Frankfurt, 1974

J.-F. Angelloz. *Rilke*, Paris, 1952

Dieter Basserman. *Der andere Rilke*, Bad Homburg, 1961

—. *Der späte Rilke*, Munich, 1947

Arnold Bauer. *Rainer Maria Rilke*, tr. Ursula Lamry, Ungar, New York, 1972

Marga Bauer. *Rainer Maria Rilke und Frankreich*, Berne, 1961

Gwendolyn Bays. *The Orphic Vision: Seer Poets from Novalis to Rimbaud*, University of Nebraska Press, Lincoln, 1964

H.W. Belmore. *Rilke's Craftsmanship: An Analysis of His Poetic Style*, Blackwell, 1954

Maurice Betz. *Rilke in Frankreich*, Herbert Reichner Verlag, Vienna, 1937

—. *Rilke in Paris*, Zurich, 1948

Rudolph Binion. *Frau Lou: Nietzche's Wayward Disciple*, Princeton University Press, 1968

B. Boesch, ed. *German Literature: A Critical Survey*, Methuen, 1971

C.M. Bowra. *Inspiration and Poetry*, Macmillan, 1955

Brigitte Bradley: *Rainer Maria Rilkes Neue Gedichte. Ihr zyklisches Gefüge*, Francke Verlag, Berlin, 1967

—. *Rainer Maria Rilkes Der neuen Gedichte anderer Teil: Entwicklungsstufen seiner Pariser Lyrik*, Francke Verlag, Berlin, 1976

Sophie Brutzer. *Rilkes Russiche Reisen*, Stallüpönnen, 1934

Else Buddeberg. *Rainer Maria Rilke: eine innere Biographie*, Stuttgart, 1954

Gerd Burchheit, ed. *Rainer Maria Rilke: Stimmen der Freunde*, Freiburg, 1931

E.M. Butler. *Rainer Maria Rilke*, Cambridge University Press, 1944

—. *The Tyranny of Greece Over Germany*, Cambridge University Press, 1935

Heinrich Cammerer. *Rainer Maria Rilke Duineser Elegien*, Stuttgart, 1937

Timothy Casey. *Rainer Maria Rilke: A Centenary Essay*, Macmillan, 1975

Eva Cassirer-Solmitz. *Rainer Maria Rilke*, Heidelberg, 1957

Fritz Dehn. *Rainer Maria Rilke und Sein Werk*, Leipzig, 1934

Paul de Man. *Allegories of Reading: Figural Language in Rousseau, Nietzsche, Rilke, and Proust*, Yale University Press, 1979

Peter Demetz. *René Rilkes Prager Jahre*, Düsseldorf, 1953

Robert Faesi. *Rainer Maria Rilke*, Zurich, 1921

Marc Froment-Meurice. *Solitudes From Rimbaud to Heidegger*, tr. Peter Walsh, State University of New York Press, 1995

J. Gebser. *Rilke und Spanien*, Zurich, 1945

Claire Goll. *Rilke et les femmes*, Paris, 1955

W.L. Graff. *Rainer Maria Rilke: Creative Anguish of a Modern Poet*, Princeton University Press, New Jersey, 1956

Roman Guardini. *Rilke's Duino Elegies: An Interpretation*, tr. K.G. Knight, Darwen Finlayson, 1961

Werner Günther. *Weltinnenraum: Die Dichtung Rainer Maria Rilke*, Berlin, 1952

Michael Hamburger. *Reason and Energy: Studies in German Literature*, Weidenfeld & Nicolson, 1970

—. *Testimonies: Selected Shorter Prose, 1950-1987*, Carcanet, 1989

—. *Collected Poems, 1941-1994*, Anvil Press Poetry, 1995

—. *The Truth of Poetry*, Anvil Press Poetry, 1996

G. Hartman. *The Unmediated Vision: An Interpretation of Wordsworth, Hopkins, Rilke and Valéry*, Yale University Press, 1954

Magda von Hattingberg. *Rilke und Benvenuta*, Vienna, 1943

Erich Heller. *The Disinherited Mind*, Bowes & Bowes, 1971

H.E. Holthusen. *Rilke*, tr. J.P. Stern, Bowes & Bowes, 1952

—. *Rainer Maria Rilke in Selbstzeugnissen und Dokumenten*, Hamburg, 1967

—. *Der späte Rilke*, Zurich, 1949

—. *Rilkes Sonnets an Orpheus*, Munich, 1937

Joachim Huppelsberg. *Rainer Maria Rilke: Biographie*, Munich, 1949

Klaus W. Jonas. "Rainer Maria Rilkes Handschriften", *Philobiblon*, xv, 1/2, 1971

—. "Rilke und Paul Thun-Hohenstein", *Jahrbuch des Wiener Goethe-Vereins*, 79, 1975

Rudolf Kassner. *Rilke: Gesammelte Erinnerungen*, ed. Klaus Bohenenkamp, Pfullingen, 1976

Katharina Kippenberg. *Rainer Maria Rilke: ein Beitrag*, Zurich, 1948

—. *Rainer Maria Rilkes Duineser Elegien und Sonnette an Orpheus*, Wiesbaden, 1946

F. Klatt. *Rainer Maria Rilke*, Vienna, 1949

Hertha Koenig. *Rilkes Mutter*, Pfullingen, 1963

Sarah Kofman. *The Enigma of Woman: Woman in Freud's Writings*, Cornell University Press, Ithaca, 1985

Werner Kohlschmidt. *Rainer Maria Rilke*, Lübeck, 1948

H. Kreutz. *Rilkes Duineser Elegien*, Munich, 1950

Wolf Leppmann. *Rilke: A Life*, tr. Russell M. Stochman, Fromm International Publishing Corporation, New York, 1984

Angela Livingstone. *Lou Andreas-Salomé: Her Life and Works*, Moyer Bell, New York, 1984

Siegried Mandel. *Rainer Maria Rilke: The Poetic Instinct*, Southern Illinois University Press, Carbondale, 1965

Eudo C. Mason. *Rilke*, Oliver & Boyd, 1963

—. *Rilke's Apotheosis: A Survey of Representative Recent Publications on the Work and Life of Rainer Maria Rilke*, Blackwell, 1938

—. *Rilke, Europe, and the English-Speaking World*, Cambridge University Press, 1961

—. *Rilke und Goethe*, Cologne, 1938

—. *Lebenshaltung und Symbolik bei Rainer Maria Rilke*, Weimar, 1939

—. *Rainer Maria Rilke: sein leben und seine Werk*, Göttingen, 1964

Keith M. May. *Nietzsche and Modern Literature: Themes in Yeats, Rilke, Mann and Lawrence*, Macmillan, 1988

B.J. Morse. "Rainer Maria Rilke and the Occult", *Journal of Experimental Metaphysics*, 1945/46

Paul Obermuller *et al*, eds. *Katalog der Rilke – Sammlung von Richard von Mises*, Frankfurt, 1966

Federico Olivero. *Rainer Maria Rilke: A Study in Poetry and Mysticism*, Cambridge University Press, 1931

Christian Osann. *Rainer Maria Rilke: Der Weg eines Dichters*, Zurich, 1941

H.F. Peters. *Rainer Maria Rilke: Masks and the Man*, University of Washington Press, Seattle, 1960

Richard Petit. *Rainer Maria Rilke in und nach Worpswede*, Worpswede, 1983

Ernst Pfeiffer. "Rilke und die Psychoanalyse", *Litteraturwiss, Jahrbuch der Görresgesellschaft*, 17, 1976

—. ed. *Lou Andreas-Salomé: Einstragungen, letzte Jahre*, Frankfurt, 1982

Donald Prater. *A Ringing Glass: The Life of Rainer Maria Rilke*, Clarendon Press, 1994

Rilke en Valais, Suisse Romande, 3, 4, 1939

Rilke et la France, Hommages et souvenirs, Paris, 1943

Walter Ritzer. *Rainer Maria Rilke*, Vienna, 1951

William Rose & Gertrude Craig Houstosn. *Rainer Maria Rilke: Aspects of His Mind and Poetry*, 1938

Ingeborg Schnack. *Rilkes Leben im Werk und Bild*, Insel Verlag, Wiesbaden, 1957

—. ed. *Rainer Maria Rilke: Chronik seines Lebens und seines Werkes*, Frankfurt, 1975

Elizabeth Sewell. *The Structure of Poetry*, Routledge & Kegan Paul, 1951

—. *The Orphic Voice: Poetry and Natural History*, Routledge, 1961

R. Schröder. *Rainer Maria Rilke*, Zurich, 1952

Carl Sieber. *René Rilke: Die Jugend Rainer Maria Rilke*, Leipzig, 1932

André Silvaire. *Rainer Maria Rilke: Inédits, études et notes*, Paris, 1952

Erich Simmenauer. *Rainer Maria Rilke: Legende und Mythos*, Berne, 1953

Jacob Steiner. *Rilkes Duineser Elegien*, Munich, 1969

Anthony Stephens. *Rainer Maria Rilke's Gedichte an die Nacht: an essay in interpretation*, Cambridge University Press, 1972

Joachim W. Storck. *Rainer Maria Rilke als Brieschreiber*, Freiburg, 1957

Fürstin Marie von Thurn und Taxis-Hohenlohe. *Erinnerungen an Rainer Maria Rilke*, Insel-Bücherei, Frankfurt, 1966

F.W. van Heerikhuizen. *Rainer Maria Rilke: His Life and Work*, 1951

Franz Werfel. "Begegnungen mit Rilke", *Sudentenland*, 18, 1976

Helmut Wocke. *Rilke und Italien*, Giesen, 1940

Heinrich Wohltmann. *Rainer Maria Rilke in Worpswede*, Hamburg, 1952

Frank Wood. *Rainer Maria Rilke: The Ring of Forms*, University of Minnesota Press, Minneapolis, 1958

Nora Wydenbruck. *Rilke: Man and Poet: A Biographic Study*, John Lehmann, 1949

Paul Zech. *Rainer Maria Rilke*, Dresden, 1930

Maurice Zermatten. *Les Dernières annés de Rainer Maria Rilke*, Fribourg, 1975

—. *Der Ruf der Stile: Rilkes Walliser Jahre*, Zurich, 1954

—. *Les Années valaisannes de Rilke*, Sierre, 1951

S. Zweig. *Abscheid von Rilke*, Tübingen, 1927

CRESCENT MOON PUBLISHING

ARTS, PAINTING, SCULPTURE

The Art of Andy Goldsworthy: Complete Works
Andy Goldsworthy: Touching Nature
Andy Goldsworthy in Close-Up
Andy Goldsworthy: Pocket Guide
Andy Goldsworthy In America
Land Art: A Complete Guide
The Art of Richard Long: Complete Works
Richard Long: Pocket Guide
Land Art In the UK
Land Art in Close-Up
Land Art In the U.S.A.
Land Art: Pocket Guide
Installation Art in Close-Up
Minimal Art and Artists In the 1960s and After
Colourfield Painting
Land Art DVD, TV documentary
Andy Goldsworthy DVD, TV documentary
The Erotic Object: Sexuality in Sculpture From Prehistory to the Present Day
Sex in Art: Pornography and Pleasure in Painting and Sculpture
Postwar Art
Sacred Gardens: The Garden in Myth, Religion and Art
Glorification: Religious Abstraction in Renaissance and 20th Century Art
Early Netherlandish Painting
Leonardo da Vinci
Piero della Francesca
Giovanni Bellini
Fra Angelico: Art and Religion in the Renaissance
Mark Rothko: The Art of Transcendence
Frank Stella: American Abstract Artist
Jasper Johns
Brice Marden
Alison Wilding: The Embrace of Sculpture
Vincent van Gogh: Visionary Landscapes
Eric Gill: Nuptials of God
Constantin Brancusi: Sculpting the Essence of Things
Max Beckmann
Caravaggio
Gustave Moreau
Egon Schiele: Sex and Death In Purple Stockings
Delizioso Fotografico Fervore: Works In Process 1
Sacro Cuore: Works In Process 2
The Light Eternal: J.M.W. Turner
The Madonna Glorified: Karen Arthurs

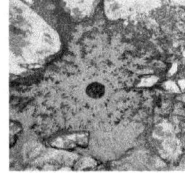

LITERATURE

J.R.R. Tolkien: The Books, The Films, The Whole Cultural Phenomenon
J.R.R. Tolkien: Pocket Guide
Tolkien's Heroic Quest
The *Earthsea* Books of Ursula Le Guin
Beauties, Beasts and Enchantment: Classic French Fairy Tales
German Popular Tales by the Brothers Grimm
Philip Ullman and *His Dark Materials*
Sexing Hardy: Thomas Hardy and Feminism
Thomas Hardy's *Tess of the d'Urbervilles*
Thomas Hardy's *Jude the Obscure*
Thomas Hardy: The Tragic Novels
Love and Tragedy: Thomas Hardy
The Poetry of Landscape in Hardy
Wessex Revisited: Thomas Hardy and John Cowper Powys
Wolfgang Iser: Essays and Interviews
Petrarch, Dante and the Troubadours
Maurice Sendak and the Art of Children's Book Illustration
Andrea Dworkin
Cixous, Irigaray, Kristeva: The *Jouissance* of French Feminism
Julia Kristeva: Art, Love, Melancholy, Philosophy, Semiotics and Psychoanalysis
Hélene Cixous I Love You: The *Jouissance* of Writing
Luce Irigaray: Lips, Kissing, and the Politics of Sexual Difference
Peter Redgrove: Here Comes the Flood
Peter Redgrove: Sex-Magic-Poetry-Cornwall
Lawrence Durrell: Between Love and Death, East and West
Love, Culture & Poetry: Lawrence Durrell
Cavafy: Anatomy of a Soul
German Romantic Poetry: Goethe, Novalis, Heine, Hölderlin
Feminism and Shakespeare
Shakespeare: Love, Poetry & Magic
The Passion of D.H. Lawrence
D.H. Lawrence: Symbolic Landscapes
D.H. Lawrence: Infinite Sensual Violence
Rimbaud: Arthur Rimbaud and the Magic of Poetry
The Ecstasies of John Cowper Powys
Sensualism and Mythology: The Wessex Novels of John Cowper Powys
Amorous Life: John Cowper Powys and the Manifestation of Affectivity (H.W. Fawkner)
Postmodern Powys: New Essays on John Cowper Powys (Joe Boulter)
Rethinking Powys: Critical Essays on John Cowper Powys
Paul Bowles & Bernardo Bertolucci
Rainer Maria Rilke
Joseph Conrad: *Heart of Darkness*
In the Dim Void: Samuel Beckett
Samuel Beckett Goes into the Silence
André Gide: Fiction and Fervour
Jackie Collins and the Blockbuster Novel
Blinded By Her Light: The Love-Poetry of Robert Graves
The Passion of Colours: Travels In Mediterranean Lands
Poetic Forms

POETRY

Ursula Le Guin: Walking In Cornwall
Peter Redgrove: Here Comes The Flood
Peter Redgrove: Sex-Magic-Poetry-Cornwall
Dante: Selections From the *Vita Nuova*
Petrarch, Dante and the Troubadours
William Shakespeare: *The Sonnets*
William Shakespeare: Complete Poems
Blinded By Her Light: The Love-Poetry of Robert Graves
Emily Dickinson: Selected Poems
Emily Brontë: Poems
Thomas Hardy: Selected Poems
Percy Bysshe Shelley: Poems
John Keats: Selected Poems
D.H. Lawrence: Selected Poems
Edmund Spenser: Poems
Edmund Spenser: *Amoretti*
John Donne: Poems
Henry Vaughan: Poems
Sir Thomas Wyatt: Poems
Robert Herrick: Selected Poems
Rilke: Space, Essence and Angels in the Poetry of Rainer Maria Rilke
Rainer Maria Rilke: Selected Poems
Friedrich Hölderlin: Selected Poems
Arseny Tarkovsky: Selected Poems
Novalis: *Hymns To the Night*
Paul Verlaine: Selected Poems
Arthur Rimbaud: Selected Poems
Arthur Rimbaud: *A Season in Hell*
Arthur Rimbaud and the Magic of Poetry
D.J. Enright: By-Blows
Jeremy Reed: Brigitte's Blue Heart
Jeremy Reed: Claudia Schiffer's Red Shoes
Gorgeous Little Orpheus
Radiance: New Poems
Crescent Moon Book of Nature Poetry
Crescent Moon Book of Love Poetry
Crescent Moon Book of Mystical Poetry
Crescent Moon Book of Elizabethan Love Poetry
Crescent Moon Book of Metaphysical Poetry
Crescent Moon Book of Romantic Poetry
Pagan America: New American Poetry

MEDIA, CINEMA, FEMINISM and CULTURAL STUDIES

J.R.R. Tolkien: The Books, The Films, The Whole Cultural Phenomenon
J.R.R. Tolkien: Pocket Guide
The *Lord of the Rings* Movies: Pocket Guide
The Cinema of Hayao Miyazaki
Hayao Miyazaki: *Princess Mononoke*: Pocket Movie Guide
Hayao Miyazaki: *Spirited Away*: Pocket Movie Guide
Tim Burton
Ken Russell
Ken Russell: *Tommy*: Pocket Movie Guide
The Ghost Dance: The Origins of Religion
The Peyote Cult
Cixous, Irigaray, Kristeva: The *Jouissance* of French Feminism
Julia Kristeva: Art, Love, Melancholy, Philosophy, Semiotics and Psychoanalysis
Luce Irigaray: Lips, Kissing, and the Politics of Sexual Difference
Hélène Cixous I Love You: The *Jouissance* of Writing
Andrea Dworkin
'Cosmo Woman': The World of Women's Magazines
Women in Pop Music
Discovering the Goddess (Geoffrey Ashe)
The Poetry of Cinema
The Sacred Cinema of Andrei Tarkovsky
Andrei Tarkovsky: Pocket Guide
Andrei Tarkovsky: *Mirror*: Pocket Movie Guide
Andrei Tarkovsky: *The Sacrifice*: Pocket Movie Guide
Walerian Borowczyk: Cinema of Erotic Dreams
Jean-Luc Godard: The Passion of Cinema
Jean-Luc Godard: *Hail Mary*: Pocket Movie Guide
Jean-Luc Godard: *Contempt*: Pocket Movie Guide
Jean-Luc Godard: *Pierrot le Fou*: Pocket Movie Guide
John Hughes and Eighties Cinema
Ferris Bueller's Day Off: Pocket Movie Guide
Jean-Luc Godard: Pocket Guide
The Cinema of Richard Linklater
Liv Tyler: Star In Ascendance
Blade Runner and the Films of Philip K. Dick
Paul Bowles and Bernardo Bertolucci
Media Hell: Radio, TV and the Press
An Open Letter to the BBC
Detonation Britain: Nuclear War in the UK
Feminism and Shakespeare
Wild Zones: Pornography, Art and Feminism
Sex in Art: Pornography and Pleasure in Painting and Sculpture
Sexing Hardy: Thomas Hardy and Feminism

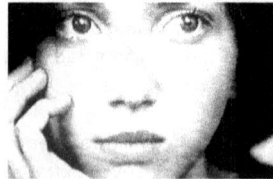

In my view *The Light Eternal* is among the very best of all the material I read on Turner. (Douglas Graham, director of the Turner Museum, Denver, Colorado)

The Light Eternal is a model monograph, an exemplary job. The subject matter of the book is beautifully organised and dead on beam. (Lawrence Durrell)

It is amazing for me to see my work treated with such passion and respect. (Andrea Dworkin)

CRESCENT MOON PUBLISHING
P.O. Box 1312, Maidstone, Kent, ME14 5XU, Great Britain. www.crmoon.com